Diesel Modeler's Guide
Volume 1

**Photos, Drawings and Projects
for the Diesel Modeler**

Contributions from

David Hussey, Randall B. Lee, Patrick Lawson
George Melvin, Rich Picariello, Larry J. Puckett
Jim Six, Jim Teese & Stuart Thayer

Scale Drawings by

Jeffrey W. Capps

Compiled and Edited by

Randall B. Lee

From the publishers of
Model Railroading magazine

Highlands Station, Inc.
Aurora, CO

Introduction

Diesels first began appearing on American railroads over 65 years ago. And it wasn't long thereafter that they began to appear on model railroaders' layouts. Although frequently prized as collectibles today, those early replicas of diesel-electric locomotives are quite crude by today's standards. The tide began to turn in the 1950s with the growing use of injection-molding techniques that made it possible to offer fairly accurate models at a reasonable price.

But for most modelers, diesels continued to be considered "all alike" for at least another 20 years. Oh, to be sure, modelers recognized the differences between E and F units and Geeps and SDs among EMD products and FAs, PAs and RSs for ALCo products along with other less-common, but very distinctive, units from other manufacturers, but many, if not most, would have been hard-pressed to recognize the difference between an F3 and an F7. And you could virtually forget any modeler knowing about phase differences.

But time marches on, and modelers have become far more discriminating. Working hand-in-hand with modelers' demands and expectations, the manufacturers that supply us with the model products we need have continued to improve the quantity and quality of models and detailing parts to make it possible for us to create as accurate a model as each of us sees fit. Whether our interests lie in first-generation or contemporary diesels, the models and parts necessary to recreate a prototype in HO scale are available more often than not. And new products continue to appear, further expanding the possibilities.

As depicted by the cover, Volume 1 of the *Diesel Modeler's Guide* starts off with a look at the NW2 and the roads that used them. The pages that follow provide the reader with useful prototype information as well as tips, techniques and insights from noted modelers on a variety of locomotives from roads across the continent. All of the articles were originally published in 1994 and 1995 issues of *Model Railroading* magazine. The articles have been grouped by railroad and compiled to provide a handy reference guide for the diesel modeler.

The cover photo of Western Pacific NW2 608 shows the prototype locomotive as it has been restored and preserved by The Feather River Rail Society for display at the Portola Railroad Museum in Portola, CA. The efforts of organizations like these play an important role in the preservation of railroad history. But they are not alone. Modelers who recreate these locomotives in miniature are also doing their part in preserving the heritage of the rails.

Randy

Randy Lee
Editor/Publisher

Diesel Modeler's Guide, Volume 1
Table of Contents

FRONT COVER: Prototype WP EMD NW2 at the Portola Railroad Museum in Portola, CA. *Photo by Randy Lee.*
BACK COVER: Model photos by David Hussey and Jim Six.

Finally...the NW2! (Part 1)

A Look at the Prototype and the Roads That Used Them

by George Melvin

*Photos by the author
unless otherwise indicated*

As our editor Randy wisely observed in "The Sandhouse" in the September 1993 issue, while discussing Life-Like's new E8/E9 model, many of the recently released diesel models have been popular with modelers and railfans but have existed in limited numbers in the prototype. The BL2, of which only 58 were built during its single year of production, is the best example of this condition. The model by Life-Like, both in HO and N scale, is a great model — but I believe I've seen at least 58 of these for sale at a single train show!

Recent introductions by Walthers of the FM H10-44 and EMD SW1 are most welcome, but again, the prototype engines enjoyed only limited sales and distribution (531 FMs and just over 600 SW1s). The NW2, on the other hand, was the second most popular switcher built, with about 1,150 units constructed during its ten-year run. It was outsold only by the ALCo S2, of which 1,825 units were built during its run which nearly paralleled the NW2 production. Forces outside the industry influenced these production numbers, as the War Production Board during World War II dictated that EMD would build only road diesels and ALCo only switch engines during 1942-1945. Alco's S2 may have won by handicap, but the increased experience that EMD got with road engines probably furthered their success after the war, but that's another story. Nonetheless, buyers of the NW2 before the 1942 edict must have been impressed; the majority bought postwar NW2s and continued buying EMD SW7/9 models after 1950 in quantities about twice that of the ALCo S4, which also began production in 1950. Now that we have models out of most of the losers, the NW2 finally represents a winner in the prototype arena!

The introduction of a prewar Phase I NW2 in a high-quality plastic model will allow the modeler of the early-diesel/late-steam era of practically any road to have that diesel switcher "nestled" among the steamers at the roundhouse. If your favorite road didn't have early S2s, it probably had these NW2s.

ACL 600 was that road's first NW2, a Phase I built in 1940. Originally painted in the famous purple-and-silver scheme, this unit is wearing the black and yellow adopted in 1967. Note loudspeaker beside headlight, box mounted on handrail stanchion (probably for flagging equipment), rerailer brackets above rear trunk and stack extensions. Florence, SC; September 9, 1962. Decals: Microscale 87-768.

James H. Wade photo, Lou Marre collection

The NW2, along with the SW1, introduced the EMD 567 engine in switcher production; the prewar NW2 using a 12-cylinder 567 and the postwar unit a 12-cylinder 567A (the SW1 has an 8-cylinder engine). The model designation is a carry-over from the Winton-powered NW1 — the "N" stands for "nine-hundred horsepower," that of the NW1 and the "W" for "welded frame," which replaced a cast frame in 1936. Other features introduced with the NW2 were MU capability as a standard option and a cabless booster version to make two- or three-unit transfer sets, commonly called "cow-calves." The TR model cow-calf was the parallel to the NW2. Watch for a future article on cow-calf units.

The diesel gurus of *Extra 2200 South* have identified five distinct groups or phases within NW2 production. The Kato model of the Phase I unit is a good choice for a model, as the Phase II differs only in two small areas: 1) The Phase I was delivered with earlier Winton-style short stacks. These were modified with extensions or replaced with the now very familiar tall conical stacks which were standard on the Phase II. 2) The Phase II, unlike the Phase I, had the frame corners slightly rounded. Since both style of

stacks are included as separate castings, and making the frame change is a simple matter, the new model is appropriate for both phases and all prewar production, as the Phase II continued in production until late 1946.

The new model exhibits some excellent detailing, including, as mentioned above, a choice of stack styles, as well as a turned-brass bell with choice of two types of hangers. The casting detail is so fine, it may take a magnifier to fully appreciate it; there is prototypically correct safety treading, two styles in the proper areas of the walkways. The sand filler even has "SAND" legibly cast into it! The handrails are thinner than previous Kato offerings and will probably be acceptable for most modelers. The model features crisper handrail bolt detailing; the bolt is cast on the body and the railing slides into a hole at the bolt end. This produces an advance in detailing but may create a bit of fussy work where a particular unit has handrails in a different color than the body of the unit. The hood-side handrails are another distinctive detail. They are cast in sections which is the type used on switchers until SW9 production began in late 1950. These were necessary to allow for the top-hinged hood doors to be opened individually.

AT&SF 2408, a Phase I built in 1939 carries a number of distinctive modifications: Window awnings side and front, homemade stack extensions and an unusual radio antenna. The "Better Freight Handling" poster on the cab is an interesting touch on this unit, which was not modified with hood louvers. Chicago, IL; November 1, 1964. Decals: Microscale 87-248.

Photographer unknown,
George Melvin collection

B&O 9515, a Phase II unit built in 1949, illustrates the 1960s simplified lettering of the road's blue-and-yellow scheme. Note furled radiator curtain, cast "F" welded to the frame and the steps and handrail next to the cab for roof access. Lima, OH; April 17, 1972. Decals: Microscale 87-401 (herald and numbers) and 87-4053 (initials).

Tim Colbert photo,
George Melvin collection

B&O 9526 exhibits the straight-sloped hood of a Phase V unit but still has the frame falsies of the Phase IV. It bears more conventional grabirons for roof access. This is the as-delivered scheme for this unit. East St. Louis, IL; August 1966. Decals: Microscale 87-52.

W. C. Thurman photo,
George Melvin collection

Postwar production of the NW2 is marked by the introduction of the Phase II sub-model in mid 1945, with the two visible changes from the Phase I mentioned previously and the change to the 567A engines used through the balance of NW2 production. In late 1946, a major spotting feature, the placing of six rows of louvers in the hood side was started and marks Phase III production which spanned about a year, to fall 1947. A cosmetic change, probably just for style, marks Phase IV production. A 12″ gap was made in the rows of louvers to provide an area for lettering. Again, after about one year, in early 1949, the final Phase V NW2 began

production with two major distinguishing features; the flat hood area in front of the windshield was eliminated and the curved trim areas at the frame corners were eliminated as well. Nicknamed "falsies," these were added to make the new welded frame look like the previous cast frame; in answer to sentiment at the time that the welded frame might not be as durable as the proven cast frame. EMD must have decided after over a decade of operation with the welded frames, that the critics had been silenced!

This brings the NW2 production up to when it appeared more like the SW7 than it did to the early NW2. A major change that

appeared with the start of the SW7 production was that the size of the front radiator opening was increased to accommodate a single 54″ fan compared to the short radiator opening which housed a side-by-side pair of 34″ fans on the NW2. This feature is the key to distinguishing a Phase V NW2 from an SW7. Although early and late phase NW2s differ significantly in appearance, an NW2 can be distinguished from an SW1 by its twin stacks and full-length hood and from an SW7 by its short radiator opening.

Now...the bad news! Many buyers of pre-war NW2s modified their units with features that became standard on postwar units.

BAR 20, a Phase V built in April 1949 shows off the solid-blue scheme with yellow lettering and silver trucks and stacks. Note snow deflector in front of the horn on cab face. Northern Maine Jct., ME; July 31, 1965. Decals: None.

BAR 23 shows off the handsome as-delivered scheme. Searsport, ME; August 1965. Decals: None.

B&M 1200, their first NW2 is a very plain Phase I unit. B&M's prewar units did not receive hood louvers. Mechanicville, NY; August 20, 1964. Decals: Accu-Cal 5820H.

Frank DiFalco photo,
George Melvin collection

These modifications improved performance of the older units as these changes were made in response to problems with the earlier units. Depending on what era you model, the Phase I and II on your road may more closely resemble postwar units and make the Kato model only a loose fit on your layout. This would vary from road to road but by the mid-'50s, that popular era among modelers, the older NW2s might no longer totally match the great Kato model. Most noticeable (and troublesome for the modeler) is the retrofitting of rows of louvers on the sides of the hood. Adding them will be a lot of work and the results may only be justified for the most critical NW2 modeler. The Con-Cor NW2, a re-issue of the old Revell model, is closer to a late-phase NW2, but it is several scale feet too long. The relevance of this issue must be decided by the individual modeler. If you successfully add louvers to your Kato model, let us know how you did it. But there is still a chance you may be in luck; some roads operated their early NW2s until their retirement without this modification.

In spite of the World War II production ban, the majority of the major railroads in existence during the decade of production bought at least a couple NW2s. A few of the roads which did not invest would include the Clinchfield, Florida East Coast, GM&O, Western Maryland and New Haven. No NW2s went to Mexico new and only CN and TH&B had them in Canada.

In alphabetical order, we will examine most of the original buyers of our subject locomotive, their distinctive features and subsequent owners. In a future issue, terminal company and shortline owners will be presented. Considering the numbers and widespread ownership of the NW2, some railroads may appear to be neglected in this survey. A thorough study is beyond the scope of our magazine.

NW2 Users

▼ **Atlantic Coast Line** rostered six units, numbered 600-605 in 1955, but they carried different numbers when delivered as ACL assigned numbers to early switchers as they were acquired, mixing several different builders in the 600 series. The old steam men probably thought, "They are all diesels,

B&M 1203 was rebuilt with an engine from an E7 resulting in the unique above-hood exhaust manifold. The tapered frame corners of Phase II units shows clearly in this view. Boston, MA; August 28, 1964. Decals: Accu-Cal 5820H.

Frank DiFalco photo,
George Melvin collection

B&M 1213 was one of the few NW2s to carry a Bicentennial paint scheme; this being a variation of the then-standard solid-blue scheme of that era. White River Jct., VT; 1978. Decals: Accu-Cal 5817H.

B&M 1212-1213 show off their full road MU equipment, both styles of handrails and spark arrestors. Also note upper areas of front windows have been painted over in lieu of an awning. This medium-green paint was a common feature on EMD and ALCo switchers. These are Phase IV units built in 1949. Mechanicville, NY; August 1964.

BN 526, an ex-CB&Q Phase II unit built in 1946, is very much as built except for added handrails on the rear platform. Superior, WI; July 24, 1982. Decals: Microscale 87-25.

Roger Bee photo,
George Melvin collection

One of four rebuilt NW2U units, BN 19 is former 469, an ex-GN Phase I unit built in 1939 and rebuilt at West Burlington, IA, in 1976. It has roller-bearing trucks, a new fuel tank, an electrical box on hood ahead of the cab and an SW1500-style headlight/numberboard assembly. Added louvers, all-weather cab window, roof-mounted warning beacon and stack extensions all date from before its rebuilding. Denver, CO; May 16, 1977. Decals: Microscale 87-25.

Neil Shankweiler photo,
George Melvin collection

BN 458, ex-GN 110 and originally 5310 is a heavily modified Phase I with extra handrails, hood louvers, stack extensions and an unusual radiator shutter atop the hood. Minneapolis, MN; July 22, 1972. Decals: Microscale 87-284.

Tim Colbert photo,
George Melvin collection

BN 471, still wearing the green/orange GN scheme, has more than the usual mods as shown on sister 458. Its frame corners are not alike and neither match its Phase I heritage as GN 124 (ex 5324), indicating a rebuilding from a wreck perhaps. Seattle, WA; October 1973. Decals: Microscale 87-86.

John Henderson photo,
George Melvin collection

BN 518, ex-CB&Q 9221, represents a mostly stock Phase II unit: no added louvers or handrails. The exterior cooling pipes were a CB&Q modification. Note the lack of white stripes on the nose. Winona, MN; September 8, 1974. Decals: Microscale 87-25.

Roger Bee photo,
George Melvin collection

CN 7937, from the first batch built in late 1946, demonstrates typical CN switcher details, such as the double-barreled spark arrestors. The black-and-gold scheme and numberboards display the unit's number *five* times on the front of the unit! Edmonton, Alberta; May 13, 1967. Decals: Accu-Cal 5808H. *Bob Loat photo, Bill Linley collection*

One-year-old CN 7938 spots coal in Ottawa, ON, in 1948, wearing the early switcher livery of black and Morency orange. While all 20 NW2s were delivered in this scheme, photos of it are rare. Note standard stack and original placement of bell. Decals: None. *A. Schwalon photo, Bill Linley collection*

CN 7963, from the Phase IV group of units, bears a couple small differences from the first batch. It has a sunshade but no all-weather cab window, has class lights on the hood front and walkway-mounted handrails (with GP9-style pressed stanchions) have replaced most of the hood-mounted railing. Edmonton, Alberta; October 1961. Decals: Accu-Cal 5808H. *Bob Webster photo, Bill Linley collection*

anyway." These were all prewar units and became 20-25 at the 1967 SCL merger.

▼ **AT&SF** or **Santa Fe** was an aggressive buyer of switchers, even before World War II, probably in an effort to curb steam switcher smoke at their urban yards. Fifteen prewar units, originally 2353-2367, were renumbered in 1945 to 2403-2417.

▼ **Baltimore & Ohio** owned a total of 52 units; 12 prewar numbered 400-411 which became 9500-9511 (9509-9511 went to the B&O Chicago Terminal) and 40 postwar numbered 550-589 and renumbered to 9512-9551. Although the prewar units were being retired as early as 1963, most of the NW2s lasted into the 1970s and beyond.

▼ **Bangor & Aroostook's** only switchers bought new were four Phase V MU-equipped units, originally numbered 800-803 and renumbered 20-23 in 1954. Although seldom operated in MU together they were MU'd with road power when moved between yard assignments, mostly at Northern Maine Jct., Millinocket and Searsport. Units 20 and 21 received the solid-blue scheme begun in the early '60s; they were sold in 1970. Units 22 and 23 were never repainted and were sold in 1967.

▼ **Boston & Maine** owned 14 units, numbered 1200-1204 (prewar) and 1205-1213 (postwar), and they were the road's first "big" or 1,000-hp switchers, predating the ALCo S2 by three years. The prewar units came in a solid-black paint with the roadname in a box, a steam engine scheme. Postwar units were delivered in the familiar black with red/white nose stripes. Most received the solid-blue scheme of the 1970s with one even getting a bicentennial treatment. The last four bought came equipped with full road-style MU stands and were commonly seen in transfer and local service out of Mechanicville, NY.

▼ **Burlington Northern**, at its merger creation on March 2, 1970, became a major owner of NW2s, with a total of 105, not counting five more on subsidiaries C&S and FW&D. There were examples of every

CNJ 1060 is in the road's modest olive-and-yellow paint and features few distinctive details, aside from stack extensions. Allentown, PA; May 9, 1952. Decals: CDS-260, Herald King L-262, Microscale 87-231.

Lou Marre photo

CNJ 1061, stored at Elizabethport, NJ, in February 1969, has small stencils for the horsepower and class SD-31 on the cab. Decals: CDS-260, Herald King L-262, Microscale 87-231.

Lou Marre photo

C&O 5201 rumbles through a junction near Chicago on September 27, 1964, still in its original blue-and-yellow paint from 1949. One unusual feature of this otherwise-plain Phase V unit is the intercom mounted on the front handrail stanchion, common in the era before every switchman carried a radio. Decals: Walthers 35900.

Photographer unknown, George Melvin collection

phase and some other interesting variations which usually threw back to the original owner. Units 450-499 were GN 102-136 and 145-162, units 500-545 were CB&Q 9203-9248, units 586, 588-592 were NP 99, 102-106 and 593-595 were SP&S 40-42. They were assigned system-wide, usually in their previous owner's territory. With 22 out of 27 BN engine-assignment points having NW2s in 1973...they were everywhere!

▼ **Canadian National** was Canada's only major owner of the NW2 because of Canada's later dieselization. As a result, some diesel models were rare in Canada. Built in two groups of ten each, units 7936-7945 are Phase III and 7956-7965 are Phase IV units. Subsidiary GTW had early NW2s which saw service on the CN as well. About half of the CN NW2s were retired by the mid-1970s.

▼ **Central of New Jersey** was a pioneer diesel user, operating a boxcab in 1925 and four Winton-powered model SW units in 1929. Undoubtedly influenced by the War Production Board, CNJ ended up with but a pair of 1942 Phase II NW2s, numbered 1060-1061. Fifteen SW7 and SW9 units followed in 1950, attesting to the success of these two early units. The NW2s became Conrail 9240-9241.

▼ **Chesapeake & Ohio** rostered only a few prewar switchers; among them were four former Pere Marquette Phase I NW2s, numbered 51-54, they became 5275-5278. The numbering of C&O switchers is quite convoluted, NW2s were numbered: 5060-5079, 5200-5213, 5275-5278, 5280-5289 (ex-PM 51-57, 59-64), 5297-5298 (ex-Manistee & Northeastern 2-3), 9558-9564 and 9565 (ex-PM 58). This totals 58 units; 29 of which were still running in 1980.

▼ **Chicago, Burlington & Quincy,** better known simply as the **Burlington,** bought 46 NW2s, numbered 9203-9248, the first 17 being prewar Phase I and the balance, save the last unit, the 9248, were postwar Phase II units. Burlington added cooling pipes above the fuel tank but did not add hood louvers. These became BN 500-545 in 1970.

▼ **Chicago & Eastern Illinois** owned about 140 diesels but just 27 switchers. The six NW2s, 120-125, were the second largest group of switchers. They became 1029-1034 in 1968 when C&EI was merged into the Missouri Pacific. All were gone from MP by 1973.

In Part 2 we'll continue our look at original NW2 users in alphabetical order. ▮

C&O 9562, a Phase IV built in 1948 was ordered by Pere Marquette but delivered to C&O, resulting in PM blue and yellow but C&O lettering and number. Note add-on (and uneven) additional handrails, canvas over both front and top radiator openings, spark arrestors and both sunshade (tipped up onto the cab roof) and all-weather cab window. Milwaukee, WI; January 10, 1976. Decals: None.
Roger Bee photo,
George Melvin collection

CB&Q 9216 is a 1941 Phase I, pretty much as built except for stack extensions. Note free-standing handgrab on front platform which was replaced with the angled hood-mounted style on later units. Cicero, IL; April 1965. Decals: Walthers 40770 (has "Burlington"), Microscale 87-609 (has stripes and herald).
Dean Givler photo,
George Melvin collection

CB&Q 9228, a Phase II issue of 1946 bears few differences from the prewar units. Note class lights are mounted closer to the hood corners and a rear-facing horn is mounted on the cab roof. A rerailer is tucked neatly under the frame above the front truck. Eola, IL; August 1965. Decals: Walthers 40770 (has "Burlington"), Microscale 87-609 (has stripes and herald).
Dean Givler photo,
George Melvin collection

C&EI 1032 shows off the MoPac blue scheme with a C&EI buzzsaw herald, working in MP territory at Carthage, MO, in June 1970. It has added handrails with GP9-style stanchions and MP-style spark arrestors. This is a Phase V unit. Decals: None.
Dave Cash photo,
George Melvin collection

Finally...the NW2! (Part 2)

A Look at the Prototype and the Roads That Used Them

by George Melvin

Photos by the author unless otherwise indicated

Kato's recently released NW2 has made it possible for a great number of modelers to have an accurate model of a prototype that was popular with numerous roads. This month we continue our alphabetical look at the roads that were either original purchasers of these units or acquired them through merger. At present it appears that at least two more installments of this article will be necessary in order to make the photos large enough to show detail adequately.

▼ **Chicago Great Western**, which was merged with CNW in 1968, owned 17 post-war units, 16-31 and 42. It was their most common switcher model. They retained their CGW numbers on the CNW at first, but most ended up in the 1000-1036 series in the 1971 renumbering.

▼ **Chicago & North Western's** NW2 ownership is anything but straightforward but here is a brief attempt to outline it! Prior to merging with the M&StL in 1956, the CNW/CMO (the Omaha Road, an early affiliate) owned a single NW2, the 70, built in 1940. In 1956, the M&StL merger added a pair, 100-101, of 1939, 1940 vintage. More came along with the CGW in 1968 (see CGW paragraph). In 1971, the existing fleet of 20 units and the ex-CGW TR2A "cow" units were grouped into a 1000-1036 series with secondhand units from GTW, KCS, PLE and SP joining in; making quite an exotic stew of rather ordinary ingredients!

▼ **Chicago, Rock Island & Pacific** or the **Rock Island** went from the 1938 purchase of Winton NW1s, the NW2's predecessor to 1948 before buying ten very ordinary Phase IV units, numbered 765-774. Another decade later, three Ontario & Western NW2s came

CGW 18 is a Phase IV built in 1948 and wearing the two-tone red-and-maroon scheme. It has a large all-weather cab window and straps for a rerailer. Painted-over areas in cab windows show clearly in this view. Oelwein, IA; October 12, 1972. Decals Microscale 87-4011.

Neil Shankweiler photo, George Melvin collection

CGW 29 is in the last CGW scheme of solid orange and black and is equipped with road-style MU but not extra handrails. This is a Phase IV unit. Des Moines, IA; July 26, 1972. Decals: Microscale 87-593.

George Cockle photo, George Melvin collection

CNW 1005 started out as KCS 1101, a Phase I built in 1941, arriving at CNW in 1973, rebuilt in the form shown here. At Cedar Rapids, IA, on May 27, 1975, sporting SQUARE stacks, typical CNW added handrails, MU equipment, twin sealed-beam headlight, blanked-out cab front windows and screened openings in the rear area of the hood — just to name the major details! Decals: Microscale 87-290.

Roger Bee photo,
George Melvin collection

CNW's oldest NW2, now 1036, ended up at the top of the 1971 number series. Originally M&StL 100 (a Phase I built in 1939) now it has MU (note small light above jumper receptacle), added railings, stack extensions and spark arrestors, all-weather cab window, small screened areas cut into the hood (and apparently taped over for the winter). The "smokestack" on the edge of the hood is probably a vent for an under-hood heater, used to allow outdoor shutdown of the engine in cold weather. St. Paul, MN; January 29, 1978. Decals: Microscale 87-290.

Roger Bee photo,
George Melvin collection

One of RI's original ten NW2s, the 768 models the plain maroon paint of the early 1960s, with silver trucks and a white frame stripe providing a little relief. On a road famous for flashy paint schemes, this was not one of them! Chicago, IL; August 14, 1964. Decals: Microscale 87-18.

Dean Givler photo,
George Melvin collection

Three years after joining RI's fleet, the 4905 wears the bright red and yellow ends of the early 1970s. Note three-chime horn, firecracker antenna, spark arrestor (leftover from PLE?) and shutter mechanism on the hood top. The bars across the radiator front and the roof drip rail are also unusual. Blue Island, IL; January 20, 1974. Decals: Microscale 87-18.

Lee Hastman photo,
George Melvin collection

RI 4909, still wearing its PLE black about a month after purchase, displays the same details as the 4905 plus has blanked-over cab front windows. Blue Island, IL; January 1, 1972. Decals: Microscale 87-18 and 87-19 (initials).

Jim Wozniczka photo, George Melvin collection

Conrail 9192, is former PC 9109, rebuilt to a 1,200-hp NW2M during the Penn Central era. It sports a new fuel tank, roller-bearing trucks, twin sealed-beam headlight, new pilot and MU on a Phase IV unit. Cincinnati, OH; December 16, 1984. Decals: Microscale 87-157 or 87-627.

Lou Marre photo, Jack Armstrong collection

DRGW 100, in Denver, May 15, 1961, bears a number of added features; both styles of handrails, factory-style tall stacks, a filter cut into the second hood door and what appears to be a walkway atop the radiator area. Note also the row of reflectors along the frame. Quite a number of changes in 20 years of service. Decals: CDS-260, Microscale 87-28.

Lou Marre collection

on board, numbered 795-797, also Phase IV units indiscernible from the RI's original ten. Another 12 years passed and again used NW2s appeared; ten Phase IV and V units from the P&LE, numbered 4900-4909. This bought the total ownership to 23.

▼ **Conrail's** creation in 1976 brought together a number of railroads which all operated in the heavily industrialized (and switcher equipped) Midwest and Northeast. This produced an NW2 roster of 149 units from four roads; 9150-9194 from PC (1200-hp NW2M), 9200-9208 from PC, 9209-9239 from EL, 9240-9241 from CNJ, 9242-9247 from LV and 9248-9296 from PC. Still common in the mid-'80s, all were gone by 1991.

▼ **D&RGW** or **Rio Grande**, had one NW2, their first diesel. It was built in 1941, a Phase I and numbered 7000 for about eight months, thereafter becoming number 100. It was sold in 1968 and became Great Lakes Steel 100. Oddly Rio Grande bought no more EMD switchers (but did buy ALCo, Baldwin, GE and FM switchers) until SW1200s came in 1964!

▼ **Erie** owned 27 NW2s, numbered 401-427, with only the first three being Phase I units. The balance were Phase IV and V units built in 1948-'49. With the Erie-Lackawanna merger in 1960 came five more Phase II units numbered 461-465, renumbered to E-L 441-445. The Erie units retained the original numbers. What evidence I came up with

indicates the smooth-hooded units did not receive louvers. All but unit 403 made it to the Conrail merger in 1976.

▼ **Georgia** Railroad owned five postwar units, 901-905 and these were the only NW2s in the Georgia Group; A&WP/GA/WofA railroads. The 901 was a Phase IV unit (and Georgia's first diesel), the balance were Phase V units. They were all retired by 1983 and probably did not wear Family Lines or Seaboard System paint.

▼ **Grand Trunk Western** received 15 Phase I NW2s in 1941-'42; these were the first EMD units on the CN system and were numbered 7900-7914. In fact, the 7903 was destroyed in a wreck on the CN in Montreal in 1946! They were delivered in a solid-

GTW 7902 shows off its as-built appearance in this undated and unlocated photo; taken early enough to catch the unit before stack extensions were added, a change made to virtually all Phase I units. Decals: Walthers 51750-?.

*Photographer unknown,
Bill Linley collection*

ICG 1438 began as IC 9155, then 1005, built in 1945. After its 1980 rebuilding to SW14 1438, little evidence of its NW2 origins can be seen! The step in the hood remains despite a completely new cab, radiator assembly, modified handrails and unusual hood louvers. Markham, IL; May 19, 1981. Decals: Herald King L-253, Microscale 87-402.

*Pete Coulombe photo,
George Melvin collection*

KCS 4200 shows off a somewhat-soiled white scheme while switching at Shreveport, LA; March 1, 1982. Decals: Herald King L-181, Microscale 87-146.

*Pete Coulombe photo,
George Melvin collection*

KCS 4205, a Phase III built in 1946, is in the solid-red scheme initiated in the early 1960s. Note can spark arrestors, twin sealed-beam head-lights and tool box on the front platform. Shreveport, LA; February 10, 1974. Decals: Microscale 87-148.

*Jim Holder photo,
George Melvin collection*

Erie 413 is a Phase IV unit built in 1948 in the standard black-and-yellow paint scheme with both styles of handrails, unusual spark arrestors and two rerailers....was the yard trackage that bad? Secaucus, NJ; March 30, 1965. Decals: Walthers 49750.

Bob Yanosey photo,
George Melvin collection

Erie 418 is a Phase V unit but bears no detail differences from the Phase IV units such as 413. It has a hanger for a rerailer over each truck. Shown switching commuter coaches at Hoboken, NJ; April 9, 1968. Decals: Walthers 49750.

Dave Engman photo,
George Melvin collection

In 1965, E-L 419 was rebuilt and matched with slug B-65, rebuilt from Baldwin road switcher 1150. They are shown together at Port Jervis, NY; June 3, 1976, in the handsome gray-and-maroon scheme. Decals: Herald King L-130, Microscale 87-16.

Jack Armstrong photo

Georgia 905 is the newest of five NW2s on the road, a Phase V unit, in tattered standard blue-and-silver paint. Note the toolbox on the front platform. Augusta, GA; June 1966. Decals: None.

Photographer unknown,
George Melvin collection

KSC 4223 is a Phase V unit in a clean coat of the white-and-red scheme. Note horizontal-mounted sealed-beam headlight. Sunshades and wind deflectors on the cab windows were present on most KCS NW2s by this date. Texarkana, TX; August 4, 1979. Decals: Herald King L-181, Microscale 87-146.

Jim Holder photo,
George Melvin collection

LV 181 wears the simplified Cornell Red scheme applied beginning in the early 1960s. Spark arrestors and a sunshade are the only notable additions to this Phase V unit. Newark, NJ; May 9, 1965. Decals: Microscale 87-775.

Bob Yanosey photo,
George Melvin collection

LV 183, probably still in its original paint, has simple (and non-matching) spark arrestors. Little else is added to this unit. Sayre, PA; May 1974. Decals: Microscale 87-775.

Bob Baker, Jr., photo,
George Melvin collection

black scheme with yellow stripes and numbers and a red herald. After the war (and delivery of CN's 20 units), the GTW received nine more units, 7966-7974 in 1947-'48. In 1980 two early and four late units were still on the roster. GTW did not add hood louvers to their early units.

▼ **Illinois Central** owned 17 NW2s, first numbered 9150-9166, renumbered 1000-1016 and when rebuilt, they became 100-116. The first three were prewar units and the balance were built in 1945. During the ICG era, the Paducah Shop rebuild program in the 1970s saw ten of them rebuilt to SW13 models (and 1300-series number) or SW14 models (and 1400-series number). The other seven were off the roster by this time.

▼ **Kansas City Southern**, with affiliate Louisiana & Arkansas, owned 34 NW2s, bought new, and originally numbered 1100-1102, 1125, 1126 and 1200-1226. They spanned the decade of production from 1939 to 1949. Also bought used were five more, three ex-MILW and two ex-Soo line, that became units 4227-4231, which were added to the new number series, 4200-4226, into which most of the NW2s went, except several that were converted into slugs. Units 4203, 4205 and 4214 were rebuilt with new radiators and roof mounted GP9-style fans, rendering a look similar to UP's SW10 rebuilds.

▼ **Lehigh Valley's** first-generation roster consisted of a third more switchers than road engines, and, despite some pre-NW2 EMD switchers, they only ended up with seven Phase V NW2s, numbered 180-186. All but the 186 made it to Conrail in 1976, becoming CR 9242-9247.

Next month, Part 3 picks up with the L&N.

Finally...the NW2! (Part 3)

A Look at the Prototype and the Roads That Used Them

by George Melvin

Photos by the author unless otherwise indicated

We start our continuing examination of the roads that rostered NW2s with a bit of good news from Kato. They have announced the release of a Phase II version of EMD's NW2 to complement their already released Phase I. They are releasing their Phase II as an undecorated model and decorated for the following roads: ATSF (blue/yellow warbonnet), BN, Chessie System, Conrail, Southern, SP and UP. They are also releasing a Phase I decorated in CB&Q's black-and-gray scheme. Two road numbers for each roadname are being made available.

▼ **Louisville & Nashville** owned no NW2s prior to its merger with the Nashville, Chattanooga & St. Louis in the late 1950s. This brought ten units onto the L&N; one Phase I unit, numbered 2119 (renumbered 2210) and nine Phase V units, numbered 2120-2123 and 2240-2244 (renumbered 2211-2219). In 1969, the L&N acquired part of the C&EI; this brought three more Phase V NW2s, numbered 2207-2209. In 1971, the Monon was added to the L&N, and again NW2s were part of the deal. Units 2202-2203 were Phase I (ex-Monon 12, 13) and 2204-2206 were Phase II (ex-Monon 15-17). This made a total of 18 NW2s, but by 1982 four had been retired.

L&N 2216 is a Phase V unit from the group received from the NC&StL merger, formerly 2241. Note plate over vent in cab front, substantial bell hanger and extra framework on front platform railing. Nashville, TN; November 16, 1979. Decals: Herald King L-280.

John Paul Rhinehart photo, Pete Coulombe collection

L&N 2209, ex-MP 1034, originally C&EI 125, is in clean gray and yellow at E. St. Louis, IL, in October 1972. Notice brackets and receptacles for class lights and frame-mounted GP9-style handrails, probably added by MP. Decals: Herald King L-282.

W. C. Thurman photo, George Melvin collection

Milwaukee 666, a Phase IV built in late 1947 is wearing the standard orange-and-black paint at Tacoma, WA; August 1978. Note trademark MILW spark arrestors and roof-mounted flasher. Decals: Microscale 87-789.

Vic Reyna photo, Lou Marre collection

MP 1020 started out as Fort Worth Belt 2. It is a Phase III built in 1946 and has been heavily "MoPac-ized." Note two-position pin puller, distinctive class lights and spark arrestors, both styles of handrails and front window awnings and toolbox on the front platform. Tiny initials to left of the herald say "FWB." Also, there is shrouding below the coupler opening in the pilot. The standard MP blue is about the only thing standard on this unit! Dallas, TX; August 15, 1971. Decals: Microscale 87-74.

Dave Lustig photo, George Melvin collection

Monon 13 is shown at Hammond, IN; September 25, 1971, two months before the end of the railroad. Aside from the stack extensions, front-radiator curtain and cab wind deflector, this unit is an as-built Phase I NW2. Decals: Model Railroad Supply #100 (contact them at RR1, Box 45-M, Middleton, IN 47356).

Bill Raia photo, George Melvin collection

Monon 15 shows off a bit flashier version of Monon's black-and-gold paint, with white lettering. Note number on pilot. Again, a very standard equipped NW2. Hammond, IN; August 22, 1971. Decals: Same as Monon 13.
Lee Hastman photo, George Melvin collection

NYC's first NW2 was the 8700, a Phase II shown here at Elkhart, IN, in May 1967, already 21 years old. Added louvers are the major detail change. Also note sheet-metal herald on the front railing stanchion. Small spark arrestors and a small beacon have also been added. Decals: Microscale 87-4004.
Lou Marre photo

Nickel Plate 8 has the obligatory stack extensions and an intercom on the front platform, a substantial push pole and, hardly visible in this view, additional railing forming a safety cage on the rear platform, an NKP feature. A good photo of this detail on Wheeling & Lake Erie D-4 appears in *Extra 2200 South*, issue 87 (April-June 1988). Calumet, IL; April 23, 1958. Decals: Microscale 87-41, Herald King L-400.
Lou Marre photo

N&W 2016 has been repainted in the NW scheme of the 1970s but is showing a lot of its earlier blue-and-gold colors from the 1960s. It has received a sealed-beam replacement headlight, has an intercom and an unidentified box on the front railing. It's less than a year from retirement at Calumet, IL; May 16, 1981. Decals: Microscale 87-22, Herald King L-50.
Pete Coulombe photo, George Melvin collection

N&W 2022 (ex-NKP 22), a Phase IV unit built in 1948, still has its NKP safety cage on the rear, spark arrestors, window awning and wind deflectors as well as a firecracker radio antenna. Chicago, IL; May 31, 1971. Decals Microscale 87-22, Herald King L-50. *Lee Hastman photo, George Melvin collection*

N&W 3352 (ex-WAB 352) was the N&W's newest NW2 (a Phase V built in 1949). It was also the last NW2 on the roster, retired by Norfolk Southern in May 1985. Note pair of square covers below sand filler in hood; these were round on most earlier NW2s. St. Louis, MO; June 2, 1967. Decals: Microscale 87-22, Herald King L-50. *W. C. Thurman photo, George Melvin collection*

NP 103, brand new at Minneapolis in 1940, exhibits some interesting features: single-loop handrail on walkway corner and odd two-stanchion front railing. Also the railing does not extend down beside the steps on the right side. Unmodified stacks, vertical hand grab on front platform and large square EMC builder's plate are typical of very early NW2s. The vintage paint scheme with "DS" for diesel switcher under the road numbering is most interesting as well. Decals: Microscale 87-143. *Lou Marre collection*

▼ The **Milwaukee Road** rostered about 85 EMD switchers but did not favor the NW2 particularly; more than half of these were SW1200s. The NW2s numbered five Phase Is originally numbered 1650-1654 and renumbered 668-672 in 1960 and three Phase IVs originally numbered 1647-1649 and renumbered 665-667 in 1960. None of these eight units had been retired by 1971.

▼ **Missouri Pacific** ended up owning a total of 32 NW2s, but only three actually started out as MP units. These were Phase I units, numbers 9104-9106. No. 9105 was sold before the 1961 renumbering; the other two becoming 1021-1022. They, too, were gone by 1968. The balance were all post-war units from five different roads through mergers: Texas & Pacific 1000-1019 (same numbers on MP), Fort Worth Belt 2 (MP 1020), KO&G 1001 (MP 1027), Missouri-Illinois 51 (MP 1028) and C&EI 120-125 (MP 1023-1034). By 1980 they were all off the roster.

▼ **Monon** owned only 11 switchers; seven of them were NW2s. Three were 1942-built Phase I units, built as units 1-3 but renumbered to 11-13 in 1947. The other four were numbered 14-17 and were Phase III units built in 1947. Five of them went to the L&N in 1971.

▼ The **New York Central** System accounted for a whopping 135 new-purchase NW2s, along with 17 bought used. The NYC proper accounted for only 60 of the 135; the first units, 8700-8704 (Phase IIs built in 1946); 8750-8773 (Phase IV) and 8803-8834 (Phase Vs built in 1949). In 1966-'67, units 8794-8802 were transferred to NYC from Indiana Harbor Belt. In 1957, 17 Phase IV units were bought from the Ontario & Western, their units 114, 116-131 became NYC 9500-9516 and were renumbered 8683-8699 in 1966. Only one of the Phase II units, the 8701, made it into Penn Central in 1968, but most of the others did. Their renumbering will be covered in the PC section.

NP 105, while only a year newer than 103, has been around 27 years; shown at St. Paul in June 1968, and has received some modifications. Eight sets of vertical louvers in the hood are most notable. All-weather cab window, stack extensions with spark arrestors, rotating beacon on the cab and the more standard paint scheme give this unit a modern look. The frame corners appear to have been rounded in this view. Decals: Microscale 87-143.
Keith Ardinger photo, Lou Marre collection

PC 8692 is former NYC 8692, earlier 9509 and originally NYO&W 124; it is a Phase IV unit in full PC paint, with silver stacks and spark arrestors. A rooftop beacon and a distinctive bell hanger are present also. Selkirk, NY; November 22, 1972. Decals: Microscale 87-94. Herald King L-361.
Ray Hubert photo, George Melvin collection

The oval on the front railing stanchion gives this unit away as a former NYC Phase IV NW2, still in its original number. The bracket for the oval and the intercom and its bracket add lots of detail to the front railings. Note also an additional row of louvers added behind the stock set. The radiator curtain is fully closed in this winter view at Detroit, MI; March 1, 1973. Decals: Microscale 87-94, Herald King L-361.
Elmer Kremkow photo, George Melvin collection

▼ **Nickel Plate Road** began its dieselization with ten switchers, six ALCo S1s and four Phase I NW2s, numbered 7-10, built in 1942. Units 11-22 followed in 1947-'48; they were Phase IV units. In 1950, Wheeling & Lake Erie's only diesels, Phase I NW2 units D-1 to D-4 became NKP 95-98; they predated NKP's first diesels of 1942 by a year or two. By the N&W merger of 1964, the pre-war units had been disposed of — the 7-10 to Wheeling-Pittsburgh Steel and the 95-98 to the Wabash. The others became N&W 2011-2022.

▼ **Norfolk & Western** was still building their own steam switchers during the production run of the NW2. However, merger with the Nickel Plate and Wabash in 1964 bought the above mentioned 12 units from the NKP along with three of the four original W&LE/NKP units which had been on the Wabash only three years; they became Wabash 347-349. Wabash's three brought-new NW2s came to the N&W as well; WAB 350-352 became N&W 3350-3352. The 3350 was a Phase II unit and 3351-3352 were Phase V units. This made a total of 18 NW2s on N&W. The Wabash 353, to

become N&W 3352, was instead assigned to subsidiary New Jersey, Indiana & Illinois as their No. 1. The 2011-2022 were retired between 1967 and 1985 with 2013, 2014 and 2021 lasting until 1985. The 3350-3352 were retired by 1985 and the 3353 (NJI&I 1) was donated to the Mad River & Nickel Plate Railroad Museum at Bellevue, OH, in 1985. The former NKP, then WAB units, were retired in 1967-'68.

▼ **Northern Pacific** owned six Phase I NW2s bought new (numbered 101-106) that were built in 1940-'41 and one used unit, the 99 (2nd) former NYO&W 115, a Phase IV

Penn Central 8669 is a former PRR Phase IV unit in PC's infamous 13-D (dirty, dull, dingy...you get the idea) non paint scheme. Aside from the weathering example, note the road number is on the canvas radiator curtain. Beacon Park (Boston), MA; June 7, 1978. Decals: Microscale 87-94, Herald King L-361. *Pete Coulombe photo*

PRR 9248 is from the road's last order of NW2s; a very ordinary Phase IV unit with the sunshade perhaps the only add-on. Notice dent in area of marker light bracket! Philadelphia, PA; July 1966. Decals: Microscale 87-67. *Dave Engman photo, George Melvin collection*

Reading 103 wears the roads somber olive-and-yellow scheme, livened up by yellow journal-box covers. In fine letters, the class (DE-9) and horsepower are visible under the cab number. Note also the road number on the left side of the hood front and maintenance point abbreviation ("EA" for Erie Avenue shop in Philadephia) on the pilot. Hinged stack caps and drip rails on the roof are RDG features. Port Richmond, Philadelphia, PA; January 1964. Decals: Herald King L-504. *Neil Shankweiler photo, George Melvin collection*

unit built in 1948. All but unit 101 went to BN as 586, 588-592.

▼ The **Penn Central** merger in 1968 brought together 32 former PRR units, from four number series, to a solid block — 8647-8678. One group of NYC units, 9500-9516, were renumbered 8683-8699, just below the big series of NYC-IHB-PLE units, 8700-8834, which were not renumbered. Subtracting those assigned to IHB and PLE and four NYC units retired prior to the merger; the PC has a total of 88 NW2s.

▼ **Pennsylvania** did not favor the NW2 for 1000-hp switchers during the 1940s but rather the products of Baldwin; buying 87 Baldwin switchers during the NW2's production run; 32 NW2s were bought. Since no switchers were bought during the War Production Board ban, the hometown location of Baldwin (near Philadelphia) and steam-era loyalty were factors. Only one pre-war unit, the 5912, a Phase I built in 1942 and two Phase II units, 5921-5922, built in 1945, were "smooth-hood" units. The balance, 5923-5925 (1947), 9155-9176 and 9247-9250 (1948) were later units.

▼ The **Reading** was another property where the NW2 was outnumbered by its Baldwin contemporary. Three pre-war Phase I units, 90-92, and Phase III units, 100-104, built in 1947 were rostered by RDG. While still active in 1970, none made it into Conrail in 1976. Unit 92 was their last NW2, serving as the Reading, PA, shop switcher until CR. It is now operated by shortline Blue Mountain & Reading in full RDG livery!

Next month we conclude our look at the major users of EMD's NW2s. Jim Six will also present a companion piece on modeling NW2s for the Atlantic Coast Line and Seaboard Air Line. **I**

Finally...the NW2! (Part 4)

A Look at the Prototype and the Roads That Used Them

by George Melvin

Photos by the author unless otherwise indicated

This final installment in our look at some of the roads that rostered NW2s picks up with the Seaboard and ends with the Western Pacific. For some additional ideas on modeling the NW2s, turn to Jim Six's article on modeling SAL and ACL units, which begins on page 30.

▼ **Seaboard Air Line** owned 86 switchers; only eight were EMDs: a single SW1 and seven NW2s, 1406-1412, Phase I units built in 1942. Known for their striking black-and-red paint, SAL's standard for switchers, they became SCL 31-36, with unit 1408 omitted as it had been retired prior to the merger in 1967.

▼ **Seaboard Coast Line** had the six ex-SAL NW2s mentioned above as well as six more from the ACL, numbered 20-25; all 12 were Phase I units built in 1942. They did not receive hood louvers but at least two were equipped with roller-bearing trucks, an uncommon modernization for NW2s.

▼ The **Southern Railway**, with its several affiliates, operated a total of 70 NW2s. They break down as follows: Central of Georgia 20, 25 (built 1941-'42); Southern

SAL 1410, at age 22, has received a few modifications — twin sealed-beam headlights, short stack extensions, a radio-equipment box ahead of the cab (note conduit to antenna) and a sheet-metal sunshade. There are two positions for rerailers but the rear rerailer is missing. Durham, NC; October 24, 1964. Decals: Microscale 87-565.

Warren Calloway photo, George Melvin collection

SCL 21 is former ACL 601, in fresh black-and-yellow stripes. Roller-bearing trucks are the most noteworthy change on this unit. Hamlet, NC; August 1972. Decals: Herald King L-380.

Warren Calloway photo,
George Melvin collection

Three years after the ACL-SAL merger, SCL 32 still wears its SAL red and black and the SCL name is starting to wear off. The unit has spark arrestors atop its stack extensions, a push pole hanging above the front truck, a toolbox on the front platform, a sheet-metal sunshade and roller-bearing trucks. Hamlet, NC; July 4, 1970. Decals: Microscale 87-565 (SAL) and Herald King L-380 (SCL).

Warren Calloway photo,
George Melvin collection

SOU 1039 is a Phase III unit in its second number. It has a new sealed-beam headlight, spark arrestors, a three-chime horn cluster mounted on a bracket protruding from the cab face. Sheet-metal sunshade, small beacon and firecracker antenna form its cab details. Meridian, MS; July 14, 1973. Decals Microscale 87-32.

Jim Holder photo,
George Melvin collection

Southern 1047, a Phase III unit, leads a herd of NW2s in switching service at Lynchburg, VA; May 26, 1978. Note this unit has MU on the rear only. Also distinctive is the louvered box ahead of the cab, large roof-mounted horns and modernized headlight. Decals: Microscale 87-32.

Pete Coulombe photo

SP&S 40 is at Seattle, WA, on June 11, 1968, two years before becoming BN 593. Note two sets of handrails, rerailer over front truck, sealed-beam headlight conversion (an early date for this) and larger-than-normal horn. An all-weather cab window and equipment box in front of the engineer window also add to its details. Decals: Microscale 87-196.

Dave Ingles photo,
Lou Marre collection

TH&B 53 has some features to make a detailed model of it unusual. Kerosene markers (converted to electric) adorn the front, along with sheet-metal panels over the radiator. A push pole and heavy chain hang over the front truck. The cab has an all-weather window and canvas awning and a three-chime horn. Hamilton, ON; April 15, 1973. Decals: Herald King L-1851.

Bill Miller photo,
George Melvin collection

UP 1011 carries "The Streamliners" version of the standard yellow-and-gray paint. Other units carried "Serves all the West" (unit 1062 for one) and "We can handle it" slogan of the 1980s (1036 carried this). This unit features a toolbox, stack extensions, wind deflectors and a canvas awning. Also note extended handrails on the rear platform, evident on all UP NW2s photos I have observed. Los Angeles, CA; September 7, 1969. Decals: Microscale 87-35.

Dick Shideler photo,
George Melvin collection

UP 1051 is a Phase III unit built in 1947. Its main feature is the train indicator boards and ladders to access them, along with a large all-weather cab window. The two-position coupler pin puller was standard on UP NW2s. Spokane, WA; December 21, 1967. Decals: Microscale 87-35.

John Henderson photo,
George Melvin collection

UP 1024, all dressed up in fresh paint at age 42, switches at Seattle, WA; May 10, 1983...perhaps UP's oldest diesel at the time? Note new version of pin puller, polished brass bell and rooftop beacon. UP did not upgrade the headlights on older NW2s, a common practice on some other roads. Decals: Microscale 87-35 (plus 87-169 for heralds).

Pete Coulombe photo,
George Melvin collection

UP 1067, built in 1947, shows the rear handrail extension and other details on the rear of the unit, such as brackets for marker lights, a step and grabirons to reach the headlight assembly and two equipment boxes. Los Angeles, CA; July 26, 1962. Decals: Microscale 87-35

Leo Caloia photo,
George Melvin collection

UP 1095, their last NW2 bought, is typical except that the truck journals have been converted to roller bearing. Portland, OR; May 17, 1987. Decals: Microscale 87-35 (plus 87-169 for heralds).

Pete Coulombe photo,
George Melvin collection

bought from NKP; they became units 346-349 (not in order) in 1961; the 346 and 347 went to Des Moines Union after brief stays on Wabash. The other two lasted until the N&W merger. One of this group, former Wabash 349, is at the Virginia Museum of Transport in Roanoke.

▼ **Western Pacific** owned but a pair of NW2s, but they were noteworthy and well-traveled specimens. Originally UP 1000-1001 (their first two NW2s), they became Stockton Terminal & Eastern 1000-1001 in 1966, then WP 607-608 in 1970. Only three years later, 607 became Sacramento Northern 607. Both these units have been preserved by the Feather River Rail Society at Portola, CA.

Acknowledgments

In addition to the many photographers whose efforts have made this study possible, I would like to thank several others who helped with the considerable research that was necessary to "find" so many NW2s: Robert Baker, Jr., Pete Coulombe, Mitch Kennedy, Bob Losse and Lou Marre. Without the use of back copies of *Extra 2200 South*, this type of article is virtually impossible to compile; their consent to use this material is particularly appreciated. For more information about *Extra 2200 South* magazine, write them at PO Box 8110-820, Blaine, WA 98230-2107.

Despite somber black-and-white paint jobs, Wabash 348 and 349 are worthy of study in that they illustrate differences between Phase I units built 11 months apart. The older 348 has the vertical deck-mounted grab on the front platform versus the angled hood-mounted style on 349. Each has a different style buffer (casting holding drawbar), different style air reservoirs, push pole brackets and rerailer hangers. The 348 has had its headlight modernized. Decatur, IL; February 14, 1965 (348) and North Kansas City, KS; June 1962 (349). Decals: Microscale 87-698.

Lou Marre photos

The month it arrived on Western Pacific, NW2 608 glows in fresh orange-and-green paint. This 1940 Phase I has many interesting points: Two-position pin puller and handrail extensions on the rear (from UP), oversize stack extensions, two sets of railings, front platform toolbox and a five-chime horn dress up this 30-year-old unit starting a career with its third owner! Oakland, CA; April 1970. Decals: Microscale 87-211.

Ed Fulcomer photo,
George Melvin collection

WP 608 as it appears today at the Portola Railroad Museum in Portola, CA. The museum is operated by the Feather River Rail Society and has an impressive collection of motive power and rolling stock including both of the Western Pacific's former NW2s. August 15, 1994.

Randy Lee photo

MODELING DIXIE...
ATLANTIC COAST LINE AND SEABOARD AIR LINE NW2s

by Jim Six

Photos by the author
Prototype data courtesy of Diesel Era Magazine

Can you picture a weed- and gravel-covered yard of three or four tracks paralleling a "main" of 110-pound jointed rail set in the sand hills area of the Carolinas or maybe southeastern Georgia? Timber-related industries are the rule of the day in this scrub pine populated region of Dixie. In the yard are a dozen or so assorted freight cars — boxcars, pulp flats and a couple of reefers part the weeds. As you sit there in your Ford pickup readying your camera for some expected action, Buddy Holly sings his latest hit tune on the radio.

Within a few moments you hear a 567 powering up and a plume of hazy blue smoke rushes skyward as an EMD switcher labors to pull loads from the nearby lumber mill. As the locomotive draws closer it rocks and rolls (like the music on the radio!) as it threads its way along the ladder track and enters the yard. The train is short but interesting. Local trains around these parts consist primarily of loads of forest products, and our little switcher's charge bears this out. In the center of the cut are four enormous woodchip hoppers that dwarf the little switch engine and

the other rolling stock. Several double-door boxcars laden with fresh-cut lumber and a few empty pulpwood flats fill out the consist.

After dropping the cut of cars NW2 #602 draws closer to the camera lens and with brakes creaking rolls to a stop alongside a small gray building with a sign over the door that reads "Yard Office." It's lunch time and the crew climbs down and heads for the local diner across the street from the yard. After snapping a few frames and a friendly wave to the crew you walk over for a closer look. The place reeks of creosote and fuel oil.

This scene isn't very difficult for me to picture since I've witnessed it and similar railroading events many times. And as a model railroader I will soon be able to relive it as often as I'd like on my Carolina and Western model railroad — a freelanced pike that hypothetically existed under the Atlantic Coast Line corporate umbrella. Such is the beauty of model railroading.

Having acquired diesel passenger locomotives in the 1930s is was no surprise that the Atlantic Coast Line took delivery of its first NW2 at such an early date — January of 1940. The locomotive was tested and carefully watched by the railroad before they ordered additional copies. Apparently the test results were positive since five additional NW2s arrived on the property in 1942. Together the six switchers would lay the groundwork for SW7s, SW8s and a large

Only a minimal amount is detailing is required to transform a Kato NW2 into a model of ACL 602. A prototype photo of ACL 600 appeared in the July 1994 issue of *Model Railroading*.

fleet of SW9s that would carry the railroad into the Seaboard Coast Line era and beyond. Originally decorated in purple-and-silver livery, each was methodically repainted into the yellow-and-black scheme (shown here) starting in 1957. I have not determined if any made it into the 1960s still dressed in purple. Maybe some knowledgeable readers can help here. All ACL NW2s would last until the early 1980s before being retired after four decades of reliable service.

The Seaboard Air Line received seven NW2s in 1942 that, like their Coast Line counterparts, would last until the early 1980s — with one exception. The 1408 didn't make it out of the 1960s. It was wrecked and destroyed at Hamlet, NC, in September of 1964. (I can't help but wonder how the railroad managed to wreck a switch engine and damage it so badly that it had to be retired?!) The Seaboard units were painted black-and-red with aluminum Railroad Roman lettering which gave way in the 1950s to the more stylized lettering font displayed by the Kato model.

For today's model railroader, having first-generation diesels for the pike is no problem at all...that is, if you can afford them! Thanks to Atlas, Kato, Life-Like, Stewart and Walthers...ALCos, Baldwins, EMDs, and FMs are all available. All are excellent models that accurately depict their respective prototypes, and all run like a million bucks. In recent years these companies have offered diesel switchers to complement the variety of road diesels in their lines. Kato is the latest to bring us an HO scale diesel switcher — the phase-1 and phase-2 NW2.

The NW2 was popular among America's railroads and in fact was Electro-Motive's best-selling switch engine. Though the Kato NW2 will probably never sell in the same quantities as the competing Athearn SW7, it nevertheless has already sold well. Look at it like this, comparing the Athearn and Kato switchers is like comparing a Chevy Cavalier to a Lincoln Towncar. The Athearn model sells for about $25 compared to the $100 Kato, but then the Athearn SW7 doesn't run as smoothly, nor is it as convincing in appearance as the Kato NW2. Both have their place, but you get what you pay for.

An examination of these photos of SAL 1406 will reveal the detailing differences between it and ACL 600 that are typical of the possibilities that modelers have when detailing specific units. Refer to the prototype photo of SAL 1410 on page 21 which shows other detail differences that exist on units from the same railroad.

For most model railroaders switch engines are ideal. Face it. Few of us have the space needed for a large mainline model railroad. A switching layout can be constructed within the confines of a spare bedroom or other minimal space which limits operating room. On a switching layout (or a full-blown pike for that matter) we can certainly shunt cars about as was described in the opening paragraphs of this article.

Having all but abandoned northeastern modeling in favor of the old South, I jumped all over the new Kato Seaboard NW2! I should have bought two! Since my Carolina and Western is to be jointly operated by the Seaboard and the Atlantic Coast Line I also wanted an ACL NW2. Unfortunately, Kato doesn't offer the model in ACL paint. Oh well — so I painted my own ACL unit.

It was apparent that the Kato NW2 would be a good model even before anyone got their hands on one. The Kato reputation has been well established as a hobby industry leader. We also knew that it would be a relatively expensive acquisition. But then again, this NW2 switcher is an exceptional model. Quite frankly, if you do no more than install the parts that come with the Kato model and add a little tactful weathering you will have one darned nice model locomotive.

On the flip side, there is a little room for improvement — just a little! First of all, the railings are (still) too thick — about 25 percent too thick. How about .018 thick railings? No one can honestly deny that injection-molded railings can be made thinner. Just look at those thin grabs that come with this model. They are on the order of about .015 or .016. Even at that, the grabs should be thinner, though this would be tough to do in plastic. Why not include formed-wire grabs — preferably pre-blackened. There you have it. In all other ways the Kato NW2 is superior to, or at least on a par with, the industry's best.

Preparation of the two models shown here was one of the easiest locomotive projects I've ever undertaken — hardly worth referring to as a project. These are simple models that call for very little enhancement to match our southeastern prototypes. After closely studying my two new Kato NW2s I got out my Atlantic Coast Line and Seaboard Air Line reference books (by Warren Calloway, editor of *Diesel Era*) and thoroughly studied photos of the prototype. For me, this step is required before beginning actual work on a model. Know your prototype!

Detail items added to the ACL model include canvas cab sunshades, cab roof vent,

Bill of Materials for NW2s

ACL	SAL	Manufacturer	Part No.	Description
1	3	Detail Associates	1802	Antenna base
1	N/A		1903	Cab roof vent
3	3		2202	Drop-type formed-wire grabs
2	2	Precision Scale	39117	Train-line air hoses
N/A	1	Details West	?	Rerail frog
N/A	1		173	Air horn
2	2	Kadee®	8	Couplers
1	N/A	Microscale	87-768	ACL locomotive set
1	N/A	Accu+paint	2	Stencil Black
1	N/A		62	Weathered Black
1	1	Floquil	110015	Flat Finish
1	1	Testors	1160	Dullcote
1	1		1161	Glosscote

radio antenna base, trainline air hoses, and exhaust-stack extensions to match ACL 602 as pictured in the ACL book. Added to the Seaboard model are sheet-metal cab sunshades, a new horn (relocated to a position between the exhaust stacks), radio antenna base with conduit, a rerail frog, trainline air hoses and exhaust-stack extensions. Both models were fitted with Kadee® No. 8 couplers. Compared with other recent model locomotives that I have prepared, this isn't much detail to add, yet sufficient to identify them as Atlantic Coast Line and Seaboard Air Line NW2s.

One last detail was added to both, the effects caused by mother nature and a little wear and tear — weathering. I remain unwavering in my commitment that weathering is the most important ingredient needed to transform a model from a toy-like appearance into a convincing replica of the real thing. Weathering doesn't have to mean trashing an otherwise good model as many envision. I'll be the first to admit that there was a time that my weathering jobs left plenty to be desired. Yes...weathering can break as well as make a good model. I rest my case.

Detail Suggestions

For both of my models I used the molded-plastic grabirons that were included with the model. I now view this as a mistake and will eventually get around to replacing them with formed-wire grabs offered by Detail Associates. So, I recommend that you buy a package of Detail Associates drop-type grabs and use them instead of the included plastic versions.

The exhaust-stack extensions were made from Plastruct white plastic tube. Take one of the separate (short) exhaust stacks to your hobby supply store and try different sizes until you find the one that fits inside of the flare at the top of the stack. Do not use the tall exhaust stacks that Kato includes with the model. They are not accurate for ACL and SAL NW2s.

Kadee® No. 8 couplers offer a much more positive centering action than the more popular (easier to assemble) No. 5 couplers. The No. 8 also has a shorter shank, so the coupler does not protrude as far out from the pilot face. Both couplers attach to the metal locomotive frame the same way — a screw through the center hole into the frame! I strongly recommend that you at least try the No. 8 coupler.

The radio antenna base is cemented to the cab roof with liquid styrene cement. On the ACL model this presented no difficulty, however, the pre-painted Seaboard unit presents a potential problem. In order to make a good bond with the plastic cab roof, you will have to carefully scrape away just enough paint so that the antenna base makes contact with the exposed plastic roof. In this way paint won't insulate the two materials from each other and the cement can work as intended.

Painting Suggestions

The Seaboard model is available factory painted in red-and-black with aluminum lettering. The paint is excellent so there is no need to paint your own. All that will be called for is to brush paint any detail parts you add and weather the model.

On the other hand Kato doesn't offer the model painted in Coast Line colors — neither purple-and-silver nor black-and-yellow. Hopefully in a future release of the phase-1 NW2 Kato will offer painted models for the Atlantic Coast Line. In the meantime you will have to paint your own as I did.

Though the paint job is straightforward — one color, black, with decals added, there is one glitch you will have to deal with. No one offers decals for an ACL EMD switcher! You will have to make do with road switcher/cab unit decals. I suggest using Microscale Atlantic Coast Line decals. The difficulty is that the name ATLANTIC COAST LINE is too long and won't fit onto the hood sides where it needs to go. That is, unless you cut apart each and every letter and apply them one at a time to come up with a more accurate fit! Yep...that's what I did for the ACL model shown here. Though I'm not really sure, the lettering appears to be ever so slightly large.

Start by painting the model black. Since I didn't want a right-out-of-the-factory-paint-shop appearance, a 50/50 mix of Accu+paint Weathered Black and Stencil Black was used for the cab walls and the hood sides and front. The roof, hood top, walkways and running gear were painted with Accu+paint Weathered Black (and further lightened later with weathering colors). The exhaust stack extensions were painted Rail Brown and later weathered with a black exhaust soot color.

After all decals were carefully applied, lined up and shrunk-fit to the surface with Champ decal setting fluid, the model was sealed with an equally proportioned mix of Floquil Flat Finish, Testors Dullcote and Testors Glosscote reduced with 50 percent lacquer thinner.

Weathering I leave to you but with a few comments. My weathering colors all consist of Floquil paints mixed in varying proportions, then thinned to between 75 and 95 percent lacquer thinner, depending upon the application. Colors used for mixes include Earth, Grime, Weathered Black, Black, Rail Brown and Roof Brown. ∎

Atlantic Coast Line and Seaboard Air Line

NW2 Locomotive Roster Data

Railroad	Original Number	Second Number	SCL Number	New	Retired
ACL	601	600	20	January 1940	August 1982
ACL	611	601	21	August 1942	October 1981
ACL	613	602	22	October 1942	October 1981
ACL	603	603	23	May 1942	February 1984
ACL	615	604	24	October 1942	June 1981
ACL	605	605	25	May 1942	October 1981
SAL	1406		31	March 1942	August 1982
SAL	1407		32	March 1942	September 1981
SAL	1408		-	June 1942	September 1964 (wrecked)
SAL	1409		33	June 1942	October 1981
SAL	1410		34	June 1942	September 1981
SAL	1411		35	June 1942	October 1981
SAL	1412		36	June 1942	September 1981

NOTE: data from *Seaboard Motive Power* and *Atlantic Coast Line Diesel Years* by Warren Calloway, editor of *Diesel Era*.

MODELING A PAIR OF ELECTRO-MOTIVE GP7

by Jim Six

Photos by the author unless otherwise indicated

Atlantic Coast Line 112 and 129 ease their train past waiting Seaboard GP18 402 in this November 1962 setting. In fewer than five years, all three locomotives will be working for the same owner — the Seaboard Coast Line. However, in 1962 the Seaboard exercises trackage rights over the Coast Line's Carolina and Western Division in western and central North Carolina.

Until 1967 the Atlantic Coast Line, the Seaboard Air Line and the Southern Railway dominated railroading in the southeastern United States. From the Appalachian Mountains to the eastern seaboard, from Virginia south to Miami, virtually every community of any significance — and a good many of little — were served by at least one of these railroads. For nearly a century it had been this way. But July 1, 1967, brought with it the end of decades of southern harmony when long-time rivals Atlantic Coast Line and Seaboard Air Line joined in corporate marriage. The Seaboard Coast Line was born. Within a few years the Seaboard Coast Line took on the guise of the Atlantic Coast Line. Headquartered in the Coast Line's high rise in Jacksonville, FL, and displaying Coast Line's yellow-pinstriped black paint scheme, Seaboard followers felt abandoned.

But change wasn't to stop there. The Seaboard Coast Line marriage set into motion a chain reaction of rail mergers that may not be over yet. In the 1970s, the SCL gained control of the *Old Reliable* — the Louisville and Nashville — and together with siblings Clinchfield, Atlanta & West Point and the Georgia Railroad the Family Lines was created. A few years later, Family Lines gave way to Seaboard System when corporate SCL, L&N, CRR, GA and A&WP were all merged (on paper). The 1982 merger of Southern with cousin Norfolk and Western into Norfolk Southern drove Seaboard System and Chessie System to seek partnership, which culminated with CSX Transportation. Today, the Southeast is almost totally dominated by CSX and Norfolk Southern. Many long-standing flags have fallen.

As a young man change meant something new, maybe a challenge — it was exciting. Certainly change ensured that I wouldn't get bored. But that was then, and this is now. I'm closing in on 50 now...not 20. When the Atlantic Coast Line and Seaboard Air Line merged it meant something new, so I didn't really feel the loss of these two former railroads. I grew to love the new Seaboard Coast Line. But when yellow and black gave way to gray trimmed in red and yellow, I got a bit nervous. Then

It is October 1961 and we are several miles west of North Wilkesboro. The 112 is about to lend a hand assisting a stalled train up the steep grade that lies ahead on the eastern slope of the Appalachians. At the time, red wood-sheathed class M3 cabooses still carried the markers on most Coast Line freights.

On this day, the 129 is the trailing unit hauling interchange traffic to the Southern at North Wilkesboro. Twin headlight fixtures, firecracker radio antenna, yellow bell, large three-trumpet horn and grabirons are all shown. The canvas cab sunshade is sagging a bit. Note the excellent detail depth behind the screen covering the body vents.

Family Lines gave way to Seaboard System and SCL, L&N, CRR and the other subsidiary identities were erased forever. I lost a lot of interest. The foundation for my railroad likes was crumbling. That's when I said forget it and switched to modeling Penn Central and Conrail!

As the years pass I long for times gone by. I want my youth back. I started riding a bicycle a few years ago. Exercise and diet became an everyday concern, and I yearned for E6s, F7s and GP7s, not high-tech GEs. Focus has become my personal buzz word. As I grow older, it is finally beginning to make sense to narrow my focus and strive for something attainable, or otherwise end up with a little of many different things and not much of any one thing. Hence the switch to the Atlantic Coast Line and Seaboard Air Line railroads operating together, sharing trackage rights and interchange. For a little spice, interchange with neighboring roads will be added.

As for recapturing one's youth, model railroading can be real tool. For me, the hobby is like a *Fountain of Youth*. As I have explained before, model railroading can be used for time travel. (Maybe I'm nuts, but I'm also happy!) It can be used as a means for traveling back to the years of our youth by simply walking into the train room! Reality may be just on the other side of the wall, but within the confines of the train room, it is still 1960 — or whatever date you want to

make it. Not only that, we can recreate earlier times as we remember them, not necessarily as they really were. A little fantasy never hurt anyone (that I know of). I know one modeler who operates the Nickel Plate Road with SD40-2s in the late 1970s! — the NKP-WAB-N&W merger never happened in his time capsule.

Since the original Carolina and Western became part of the Atlantic Coast Line a couple of decades before my modeling period, the C&W Division should appear as just another part of the greater Coast Line. That means that GP7s, Es and Fs are a part of everyday operations on the C&W Division.

Here's the 129 running backwards! Yes, on the Atlantic Coast Line GP7s were set up to operate short hood forward. But in local service you are rarely afforded the opportunity to turn a locomotive, so if you started out in the morning short hood forward, you returned that afternoon running backward.

ACL 112 displays the first yellow-and-black scheme applied to the Coast Line's Geeps. If you replace purple and silver paint with black and leave all but the yellow stripe along the roof, you get this scheme. Several ACL Geeps were painted in this variation including the 112 and the 147. The 112 retained its curved stripes for a while after the Seaboard Coast Line merger in July 1967.

Running late the 129's engineer has her notched out and running at track speed. We don't want to outlaw. Accu+paint Stencil Black and Erie-Lackawanna Yellow paint were used along with Microscale Atlantic Coast Line decals for these ACL GP7 models. But let's admit, it is the weathering that puts the final touch of realism in this photo.

HO Scale GP7 Modeling

In this article, I'll review what it took to come up with the two Atlantic Coast Line models featured here. It wasn't as easy as you might think. The first order of business was to research the Coast Line's GP7s and decide upon which units to model. One thing that became immediately apparent was that as generic as they might appear, each locomotive had its own identity. The railroad made several modifications to them during their service lives, and the older they are to appear, the more modifications that need to be included if a locomotive is to be accurately represented in model form.

For one thing, the paint started out as ACL purple and aluminum (silver) with black-and-yellow trim. In the mid-1950s, the font of the lettering was changed to larger, "thicker" lettering. Then in 1957, both the purple and silver were replaced with engine black with most of the yellow stripes remaining in place. A year or so later, the curved yellow pinstripes on the hood ends were straightened out to run horizontally and parallel all of the way around the locomotive. My two models represent both of these variations. I am contemplating a purple unit, but as yet have not acted on this.

Another consideration is detail. By 1960 the Coast Line's classic EMD Geeps had received several modifications that were outwardly visible. Three modifications stand out: 1) the *skirts* hiding the open area above the fuel tank (on each side of the locomotive) were cut away, 2) the bell was relocated from behind the pilot to the top of the short hood, and 3) the horns were moved to the top of the short hood. Another detail (that may be unique to Atlantic Coast Line GP7s) is what appears to be a strap wrapped around the center of the fuel tank. This detail was also found on some Geeps while still in purple paint. Wanting my locomotives to be believable, paint, detail and weathering would have to be considered — within reason.

So I set out to find a good GP7 to work with. It's easy to find a good GP7 — the Atlas/Kato phase-1 GP7. Trouble is, as good as this model is, it does not lend itself to modification — like removing the skirts from above the fuel tank. Its one-piece cast-metal walkway/pilots/fuel tank cannot be modified without a machine shop. I don't know about you, but I don't have a machine shop in the basement.

Well, there is always the old Athearn GP7, but it too has the fuel tank cast to the frame in such a way that it needs a machine shop to modify. Besides, its too-wide hood throws off the appearance of the carbody. Acceptable back in the '60s, but not in 1995!

So then what? — KITBASH! Oh no, not that awful seven-letter word. Until someone offers a GP7 (and GP9 for that matter) of current model locomotive standards, if you want a GP7 to represent anything other than the earliest version, and early on in its service life, you are faced with either some serious compromising, or a kitbash project. Most modelers bite the bullet and compromise. But for me, to paint an Atlas/Kato GP7 in Coast Line black and yellow and not be able to remove the fuel-tank skirts just doesn't get it. Sorry guys, that's the way *I* see it. *(Before getting involved with the kitbashes I performed, you might want to consider getting one of the old Front Range GP7 models now available from Trains Unlimited. The only drawback is that the detail fidelity of the carbody is not as good as the Atlas. Hint. Hint!)*

For my model of ACL 129 I fit an Atlas GP7 hood and cab to a Front Range walkway and drive unit, then replaced the power trucks and drive linkage with Athearn components. Athearn trucks and drive linkage coupled to the Front Range (Mashima) make for an excellent-performing locomotive that runs well with Kato-powered units. The result is a kitbash that didn't call for any sawing, cutting or splicing. (Phew!) I pretty much created my own kit, rather than kitbash. The completed model is one of contemporary standards that runs as well as it looks.

Here ACL GP7 181 rests alongside an F7 at the Sanford, FL, engine service shed. This locomotive displays the small herald on the side of the short hood. Very few GP7s ever had the small F-unit-sized herald. Headlight color positions are clearly visible here as are many detail items that are commercially available for models from Detail Associates and others. Sanford, FL; August 1966.

The 216 and the 196 both need a paint job — which isn't far off. In less than a year both will get a fresh coat of yellow-trimmed black paint, but this time the silver lettering will read SEABOARD COAST LINE rather than ATLANTIC COAST LINE! Several locals off into the citrus belt of Central Florida operated out of the Sanford facility in the mid-1960s. Sanford, FL; August 1966.

On the other hand, my model of ACL 112 has a different lineage. To the point, the 112 is an Atlas GP7 body fit to a Life-Like PROTO 2000 GP18 walkway and drive unit. Both models were detailed and painted to match their specific Atlantic Coast Line prototypes as they appeared back in the late 1950s to mid 1960s. They are 100 percent operationally compatible, and having the Atlas GP7 bodies, are a matched set of the best detail fidelity available for a GP7.

Detailing the Models

Cab sunshades are a distinctive detail that many of us add to our model locomotives — and why not? They get noticed by all but the blind! (Just kidding.) Where many railroads used trapezoid-shaped sheet-metal shades, the Coast Line (and Seaboard) used canvas shades. To represent canvas, I cut the shades from the thin gray cardstock used in Cannon & Co. detail-parts packaging. (Thanks Gordon! I told you that sooner or later, you would do early EMD Geep detail parts!) Each shade was cut out and slightly *bowed* to represent canvas sag, then soaked in Super-Jet cement and allowed to dry. Each was then cemented to the cab roof just above the side windows. Two supports, one beneath each corner of the shade, were made of .015 brass rod and fit in place by drilling holes into the cab wall and securing them with Super-Jet.

Another detail that gets noticed is the bell centered atop the short hood. They were painted yellow! Three-trumpet air horns were then also fit to the top of the short hood. There appears to be no consistency of the type of horn used on the Coast Line's GP7s. I used three-trumpet horns, both different. A firecracker antenna goes on the cab roof. Note though that many Coast Line GP7s were equipped with whip-type antennas. Detail Associates formed-wire eyebolts were drilled for and installed as lift rings. One last roof detail was to replace the cast-on exhaust stacks with Detail Associates replacements. Why? The cast-on versions taper to the top, whereas the Detail Associates version is straight to the top matching the prototype. Oh heck...they just look better!

All grabirons were carved off of the Atlas/Kato body and roughed areas sanded smooth. Drop-type formed-wire grabs (Detail Associates or Tichy) were drilled for and secured with Super-Jet cement. Another cast-on detail to go was the hand-brake

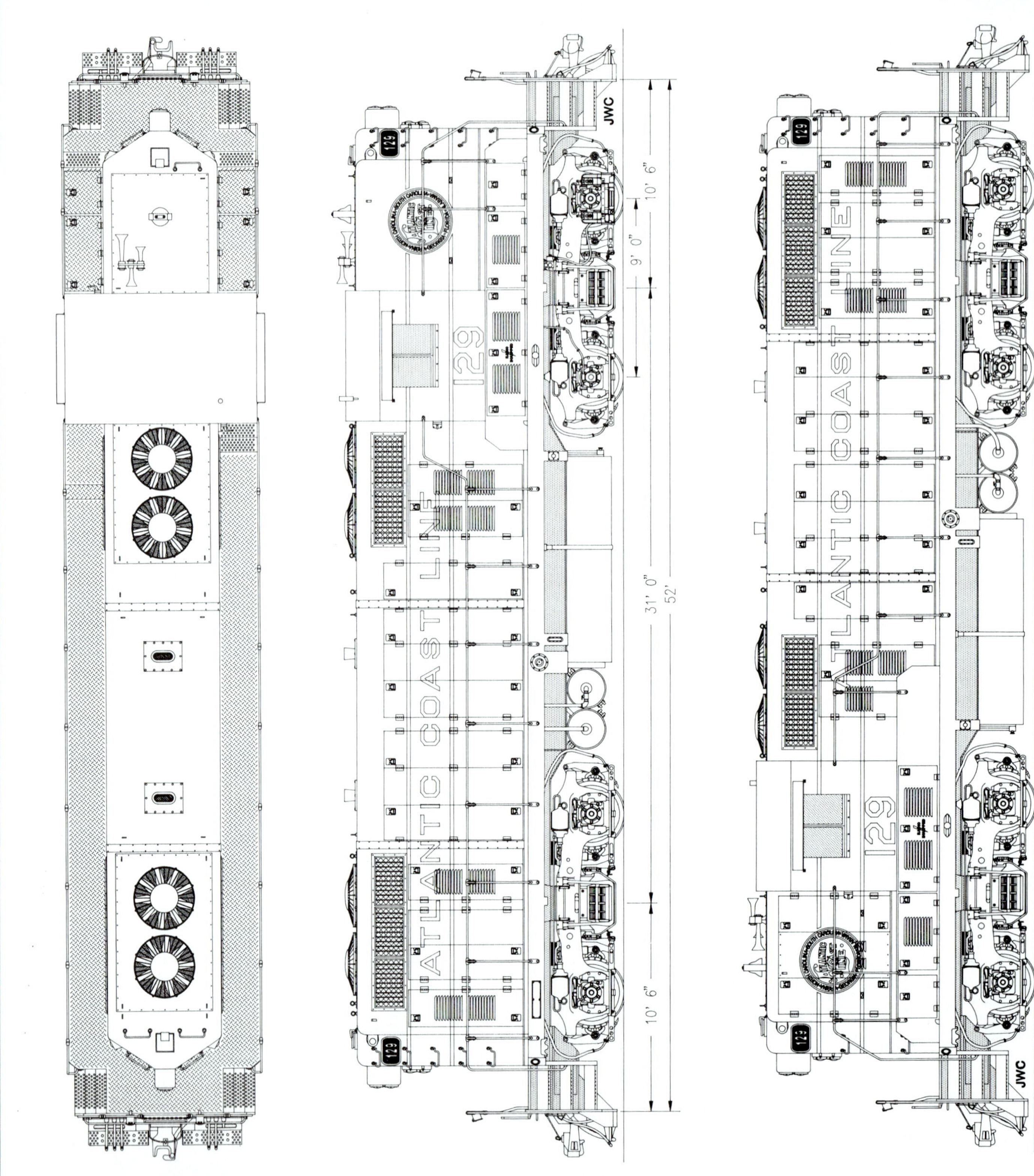

ratchet at the end of the long hood. Studying photographs, it appears that the Atlantic Coast Line GP7s did not have a hand brake on the outside of the locomotive. I assume that the units had a brake, so it must have been located inside somewhere. At any rate, that's one less detail to worry about.

The cast-on headlights were filed off and replaced with Detail Associates replacements (see Bill of Materials). The large light fixture goes on top, the smaller one below.

This arrangement goes on both ends of the locomotive. The large top fixtures get MV LS22 clear lenses above and MV LS220 red lenses below. The lower light fixtures get two MV LS22 clear lenses.

I suggest using the stanchions that come with the Atlas GP7 body. They have unprototypically thick railings, but can be cut free of the railings and drilled to accept .019 formed-brass replacement railings. There are two MU plugs at each end of the locomotive.

They are older types that are fit to LB condulettes, one flanking each side of the (Detail Associates) drop step. To represent this arrangement, I used Precision Scale GP9 stanchions inverted, then fit Detail Associates MU-plug covers to the holes where the railings would have gone. Sounds crazy, but nevertheless, very effective!

Pilot detail consists of EMD early-type drop steps, pilot-wide grabs, coupler cut levers, MU hoses and trainline air hoses.

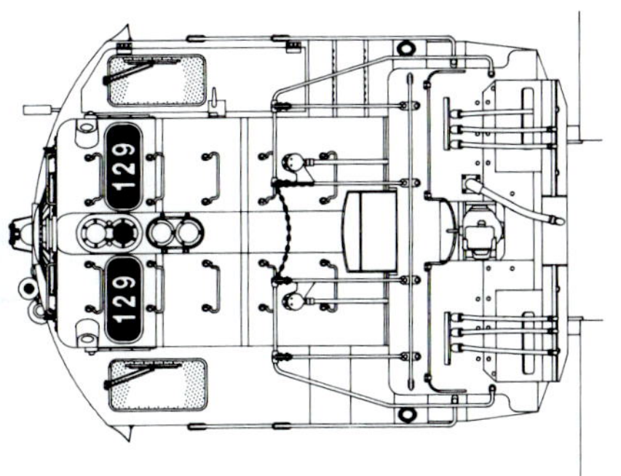

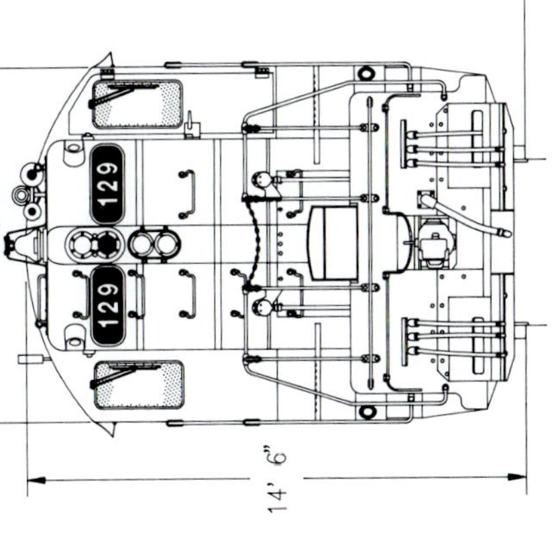

Bill of Materials

Qty.	Manufacturer	Part No.	Description
1	Custom Finishing	113	Firecracker radio antenna
1		202	ATS pickup and connector
1		221	RSL-3L three-chime air horn
2	Detail Associates	1401	Drop steps
2		1507	MU receptical covers
1 pkg.		2201	Grabirons with nut/bolts
2		2204	Coupler lift bars
1 pkg.		2206	EMD formed-wire lift rings
2		2402	Normally aspirated Geep exhaust stacks
2	Details West	116	Pyle twin Gyralight
1		128	Bell
2		148	Pyle twin flush headlights
6	MV Products	LS22	Clear headlight lens
2		LS220	Red headlight lenses
2	Kadee®	8	Couplers
1	Atlas		GP7 body without dynamic brakes
1			GP7 clear plastic window set
1	Life-Like Proto 2000		GP18, or...
1	Trains Unlimited		GP7 (chassis/power unit)
4	Athearn	42012	Blomberg B truck sideframes

Here, the 112 awaits clearance to proceed west just outside of North Wilkesboro, NC, Being that this train is headed by GP7s tells us that this is a local or secondary train. That there are two units says that business is good on this sunny December 1959 day. In those days, the 112 and the 129 were regulars on the C&W Division west of Winston-Salem.

The 112 leads GP7 129 past a Clinchfield Geep at Johnson City, TN, as it utilizes trackage rights over the CRR to gain access to the coal fields around Norton, VA. That the Waycross (GA) shops have modified this unit is apparent. Note the missing skirt above the fuel tank. In spite of the fact that the locomotive appears somewhat clean, there's some rust streaking starting to show on the yellow stripe beneath the battery box and grime from sloppy refueling around the rear area of the fuel tank. Note that the Clinchfield Geep retains its fuel-tank skirt.

Piping was added to the air reservoirs and sand hoses and speed recorder to the trucks. Straps (brass strips) were fit to both sides of the fuel tank — very much an Atlantic Coast Line spotting feature. Other than that, Kadee® couplers, paint, decals and weathering finished the models.

A close look at the prototype photos will reveal three versions of the black-and-yellow paint scheme. There was a fourth variation on the yellow-and-black scheme, which we

This is the photo that inspired preparation of the models featured here. As you can see, this early black-and-yellow scheme lasted right up to the end of the ACL and in fact is not in bad condition. There was a time when the Coast Line tried to repaint its diesels every year or so! But by this late date, this practice no longer remained in effect. Rocky Mount, NC; July 23, 1967. *Warren Calloway photo, courtesy of* Diesel Era *magazine*

Here is another GP7 that retained its curved stripes into the middle 1960s. That the fuel-tank skirt has been removed is obvious. This is a feature not readily represented on over-the-counter HO scale GP7 models. Rocky Mount, NC; April 10, 1965. *Warren Calloway photo, courtesy of* Diesel Era *magazine*

Here is a classic roster photo of ACL 154 at the Rocky Mount facility. Note the aluminum-colored cover plate over the warning light. A small five-trumpet horn and bell are atop the short hood. And again, note the open area above the fuel tank exposed by removal of the skirt. Also notice that the logo is offset a bit high on this locomotive. Rocky Mount, NC; November 20, 1966. *Warren Calloway photo, courtesy of* Diesel Era *magazine*

Other than the excellent view of the locomotives and its detail, you ought to consider the ground around the unit — a lot of silty earth discolored by oil, fuel and other grime from servicing locomotives. Also notice the sand from leaking sanding valves! Don't just detail and weather your locomotives and rolling stock; consider treating the ground with the same concern! Rocky Mount, NC; March 20, 1966.   *Warren Calloway photo, courtesy of* Diesel Era *magazine*

This is a former Charleston and Western Carolina GP7 recognized not only by the road number, but also by the small F-unit-sized logo on the side of the short hood. For whatever reason(s), most former C&WC units received the small logo in place of the much larger ones found on ACL's own Geeps. Rocky Mount, NC; September 3, 1967.

Warren Calloway photo, courtesy of Diesel Era *magazine*

will get to in a moment. The earliest is represented by my model of the 112 with curved stripes at the hood ends (outlining where the silver band on the purple carbody used to be) and a large herald on the sides of the short hood. The model of the 129 displays the most common version of ACL black and yellow with the horizontal pinstripes all of the way around the locomotive. It too has the large circular herald. The prototype photo of the 266 shows the less common small F-unit-sized herald on the

sides of the short hood. A fourth version (not shown) has horizontal stripes but without a herald. I can confirm that this last version showed up on at least one locomotive. For more information on paint schemes applied to the ACL's Geeps, refer to the Warren Calloway book on ACL diesels.

Looking over my two Atlantic Coast Line GP7s, I realize that they are not perfect. What model is? On the other hand, I haven't seen anyone do any better, at least not in HO scale. The one thing that matters

to me is that I have achieved a good level of realism at reasonable cost of time and resources. The models are believable, yet remain usable for everyday layout use without any special considerations.

Hopefully, this will motivate others to follow suit and maybe encourage some manufacturer to offer GP7 and GP9 models that are easily modified to represent these popular locomotives as they appeared at various times during their now going on 50 years of service. Happy modeling!

by David Hussey

Photos by the author

Modeling ATSF Phase I and II
GP50s

Santa Fe first purchased EMD Phase I GP50s in 1981, starting with the 3810 class of 30 units (3810-3839) delivered February-April 1981. A second order was placed for 15 Phase II units in the 3840 class (3840-3854) with the entire order delivered in April 1985. All of the Santa Fe GP50s were delivered in the blue-and-yellow Warbonnet paint scheme and came with Blomberg type B trucks with elliptical springs, 70:17 gearing, 3,500 gal. fuel tanks, extended-range flat dynamic brakes and cab-mounted air conditioners. Engines 3810-3822 were delivered with Locotrol; even-numbered units 3810-3822 were set up as lead units and odd-numbered units 3811-3821 were set up as remote units. The Locotrol equipment was subsequently removed. All were built with the 16 cylinder 645F3 prime mover producing 3,500 hp and 64,200 lbs. tractive effort at 9.7 mph and weighed 271,663 lbs. for the Phase I and 273,120 lbs. for Phase II.

On the surface the phases appear similar, but EMD, keeping up with their "Every Model Different" philosophy made several substantial changes. The sidesills on the Phase I engines are thin in the center above the fuel tank and air reservoir and get thicker approaching the ends; on the Phase II units the sidesill is one constant thickness similar to the thin center section on the Phase I. The front anti-climbers on the Phase I taper at about 80° from the centerline and have rounded corners at the side. The rear anti-climber has a sharper taper more parallel to

the rear of the long hood with a rounded tip. Both anti-climbers on the Phase II engines have the same taper as the Phase I front, but have sharp corners and the deck overhangs slightly to facilitate welding during fabrication. The Phase II units also feature the "Free Flow" angled traction-motor blower duct as opposed to the mail-box style of earlier EMD designs.

Modeling ATSF GP50s

I started this project several years ago as part of a group of Santa Fe Super Series GP units including both phases of the GP50, both phases of the GP60 and the wide-nose GP60M. However several distractions, other projects and various excuses made this effort take almost four years to complete. Mind you these are not that difficult, but... For this article I'll just cover the two phases of GP50 for now. When I start a project I like to do as much research as I can into the specific prototype. This starts with photos. I live in Southern California with reasonable access to Cajon Pass and Tehachapi as locations for shooting Santa Fe and also UP and SP. Over the years I have built up a good collection of photos. I prefer prints since they are easier to file and access for modeling projects. The local processor makes double 4x6 prints and supplies replacement film for a moderate price. I usually go railfanning with my friend and fellow modeler Ed Ryan, so when we see something of interest we both shoot it from opposite sides — that way we can

swap the dupes and get twice the coverage when we get the prints back. Engines are sorted by road, then type, then filed in three-ring albums by number. As we get more engines, fill-in pages can be added with "little" effort — ha! — we need a full-time librarian. One piece of advice, "Film is Cheap." It is much easier to shoot more photos of an engine or car you find parked on a siding in the middle of nowhere than it is to go back later and hope you can find it again. I find it hard enough to build an accurate model of modern equipment when armed with a dozen photos. I don't think I could build models based on just one old photo of earlier trains, but I respect those who can. I find it extremely helpful to have roof shots since that is the most viewed side of a model. Usually we try to find a bridge or rock outcropping to get that angle.

Anyway, armed with this collection of photos one of the first things I do is make a matrix of all the features of the intended subject. In this case the five versions of ATSF Geeps I was going to build. By studying the photos things like nose length, fan type, headlight placement, horn location and type, etc., are added to this matrix along with a possible road number. Having a specific number in mind when starting helps focus the model into a specific unit as opposed to building something then trying to find a number it matches. Working from the matrix I am able to make up a list of features for each engine and make a decision about

ATSF GP50s 3810 and 3842 are ready for their daily assignments. Unit 3810 is a Phase I GP50 while 3842 is a Phase II model.

what I am going to do with each model. For example the Phase I GP50 was delivered with Locotrol and had a pair of distinctive antennas mounted between the last two cooling fans for sending and receiving. Some top-down photos which showed that feature led me in that direction for that model; even though they have since been removed, I liked them. One down.

I usually prefer to have photos of both sides along with the top from about the same time period since we all know those sneaky railroads like to change things just to keep us off balance. With the shots I had I selected the class loco 3810 for the Phase I. The Phase II engine research focused on 3842 since I had more photos of it than any other. One problem with taking so long to finish this project was that Santa Fe kept changing 3842. I've got shots of it with a high-mounted headlight, low-mounted head-

Compare the differences in nose details in these two photos. The text describes how the variances in each were modeled.

light, with and without the air conditioner, with and without the American Flags and finally with ditch lights. It was the latest version I settled on — with the low headlight, flags and ditch lights. Lets get started.

Body Modifications

The first thing I like to do is make the major changes that require sawing and filing to the shell. That way a slip of the saw or file doesn't damage a shell with a lot of

work in it. I used the Athearn GP50 for the basic starting point. The Athearn shell represents the early Phase I design and doesn't really require a lot of modifications for the ATSF Phase I, although I did make some improvements. One of the advantages/disadvantages of taking so long to finish a project is the release of new improved parts from the various manufacturers that can be incorporated although sometimes it's too late. As an example, when I finally really got going on these, Cannon & Co. had just released their exquisite nose kits, so they were a definite addition along with the Dash 2 cab which I already planned on using.

Since these engines were built after the incorporation of the "clean cab" in 1977 some modifications are necessary to the cab and nose. In that time frame EMD changed from a water heater to an electric heater for

ATSF 3810 is a Phase I GP50 with a "notched" sidesill that is narrower in the center that at the ends.

the cab although the incorporation was done more by railroad order than EMD decision. Santa Fe had these options; therefore it is necessary to fill the louvers in the front of the cab wall under the engineer's window and on the left side of the nose near the door. A lot of people use various putties and body fillers for this, but I prefer a faster way. Thick "gap-filling" CA applied with a piece of wire and sprayed with a plastic-compatible CA accelerator such as Pacer Technologies' Kicker for Plastics hardens in seconds and is ready to file or sand without hours of drying and the resultant shrinking.

The other cab modification is the removal of the microscopic bolt heads that Gordon Cannon has so painstakingly added to the plates around the side windows. This will represent the later-production welded construction. They can be removed by scraping with the edge of a knife or razor then sanding smooth. Use care to avoid nicking the base surface. Prior to assembling the cab I find it easier to drill the holes for the windshield wipers since the access is easier now.

After the cab was assembled per Can-

non's instructions the noses were next. The Athearn shell comes with the correct length 88″ nose, but I wanted the fidelity offered by the Cannon nose. It is also easier to make the cuts required to install the repositioned low headlight. I used a Details Associates (DA) 1003 headlight casting so the cut was sized to fit it, then a styrene backing plate was added from the inside. Both engines utilize the ratchet hand brake so that nose side was used. The Santa Fe has blanked out the marker castings. To represent this, fill the holes with the Cannon gasketed blanks and sand the surface flush and smooth. The patches are made from .005 styrene cut into a .120 square for 3810 or octagonal for 3842.

As the nose was assembled, the seams were filled and dressed using another technique I came up with. For years I have used a primer that is used in the model airplane hobby called, are you ready for this, "Mr. Surfacer 1000." It is made by a Japanese company, Gunze Sangyo. This primer is the best I have ever encountered. It is plastic compatible, dries to a very thin gray satin surface in minutes when airbrushed and thinned

50/50 with their thinner, "Mr. Thinner for Mr. Color," and can be sanded both dry and/or wet after about ten minutes drying. Try a shop that sells model airplane and armor kits to locate this product; you won't regret it.

Anyway back to the seams on the nose. To fill the seams I use the Mr. Surfacer pigment that settles to the bottom of the bottle. Use a stick or piece of wire to retrieve some of this pigment and apply it directly to the area that needs a little filling such as these seams or a nick or gouge. It dries in 15-20 minutes and is ready to sand. I have been using some sanding sticks that I think come from women's' finger nail shops and have four grits applied to a hard-foam backing about the size of a tongue depressor. They work great since you can progress to finer grits without having to hunt down other tools as you go. I recommend wet sanding to get that extra smooth surface since the Gunze will show up the scratches.

Before adding the Cannon parts to the shell it is a good idea to do all the cutting. On 3810 the front anti-climber was removed flush with the pilot end plate along with all cast-on detail on both of the pilots. For 3842, both front and rear anti-climbers are removed along with the cast-on pilot detail. The original Athearn cab was removed and the nose was sawed off per the Cannon instructions. As I stated earlier some parts came out later; such was the case of the Cannon sub bases. Had they been available at the time the entire cab/nose/sub base would have been removed at this time. Later events (I'll explain as we go along) did permit the sub base to be added to 3810. The blower duct on 3842 also needs to be removed to make room for the Cannon angled blower housing. It's starting to sound like a Cannon ad isn't it, well these parts are just too good to leave off. The electrical box behind the cab on 3810 was also removed now (this is optional).

The Athearn shell has the correct sidesills for Phase I, but to model a Phase II the sidesill must be trimmed to match the center section. Scribe a line with a pair of calipers or ruler and cut/file down to the line, measuring as you go to avoid going to far. Be sure not to damage the jacking pads. At this time I also cut off the Athearn air reservoirs since they are only semi-circular.

The other modification done at this time was to the rear of the long hood. The Santa Fe does not use rear numberboards so they were filled with the Athearn insert and a combination of the CA/Gunze tricks, followed by sanding, priming, sanding, etc., until the area was smooth and flat. The marker castings were also removed as was the gasket near the top. The bolt heads for the grabirons were also lost during this operation but will be replaced later.

Although I usually replace the fans with see-through replacements, these models presented a dilemma for me. I don't really like any of the after-market "Q-fans" — I don't think they have the correct shape or center plate or both. I chose to keep the Athearn fan since my measurements and photos of it indicate, in my opinion, it is the most correct. I also removed part of the steps to represent the correct late-produc-

tion GP notched step well. I'll discuss those modifications later.

Before adding parts, I do all the drilling that will be required such as: lift rings, grabirons, MU air hoses, coupler cut bar brackets, train line and the mounting holes for the snowplow. The pilots also have reinforced slots for lifting the body off the trucks. These are made by drilling a pair of .046 dia. holes, .060 from the edge, .425 and .480 up from the bottom of the pilot. A piece of .020 x .100 x .100 with a centered .046 dia. hole is glued over the top hole to represent the reinforcing plate. After the glue dries, the web between the holes is cut out making a slot. The finished plate should extend down about halfway along the slot.

The anti-climbers are added now. I used the Details West (DW) 189 for the front of 3810. Be sure it is flush with the deck. Fill and sand the transition smooth so it doesn't show later. Add the supports as supplied. The anti-climbers on 3842 were scratchbuilt. This technique is applicable to any modern GP or SD and the result is not unique to just the Santa Fe GP50. I started with a piece of .060 x .188 x .900 Evergreen styrene. Lightly scribe a centerline across the part .450 from either end. Next scribe a line .110 from one side along the entire length. Now

In this more recent view of 3842, the area around the low-mounted headlight shows evidence of grinding from where the headlight was installed and the the octagonal class-light blanks are really obvious. Note the addition of ditch lights and that the lead radiator fan has been replaced — it's only been primed.

with a straight edge scribe two lines from the centerline to where the .110 line reaches the ends. This should result in two triangles .078 x .450 that will be removed to form the new anti-climber. One way to do this is to clamp the part in a small vice aligned on this angled line, with just the triangle portion sticking out. Use a large file and file down to the vice jaws. Reposition the part for the other triangle and repeat. You should have a "house-shaped" part that will be the basis for the anti-climber. Now add a piece of .020 x .080 x .550 along the beveled surface from the peak extending past the side and flush with the surface that will become the deck (with the scribed side down). After the glue dries repeat for the other sloped surface. When dry trim the overhang flush with the sides. Now add two pieces measuring .020 x .080 x .160 along each end, again flush with the deck and the base. Trim flush with the slope when dry and dress the joints.

Now comes the trick to represent the lip around the deck. Use a strip of .010 x .020 and repeat the above steps except this time instead of being flush with the deck surface leave one half of the .020 width stick above the surface. When this dries trim the piece sticking above the deck flush with the deck using a sharp razor or file.

You should now have a .060 thick anti-climber with the .020 x .080 fascia extending slightly below the deck and a .010 x .010 lip around the deck edge at the top, representing the deck plate overhang. Glue the completed part to the pilots flush with the deck and fill and dress as necessary to get a smooth deck

transition. Supports are fabricated for the front anti-climber only similar to the DW part from .015 x .125 x .155 and positioned at 45° between the pilot and the bottom of the deck about .050 inside of each edge.

One other feature that I noted when making the matrix is the difference in battery box and equipment-cabinet doors; the units are different from each other and from the stock Athearn. Since the Cannon sub bases were not yet available when I started, I modified the Athearn doors to duplicate the prototype. The Athearn equipment doors (the ones under the cab) have three small welded hinges and a stiffener just above them along with three latches. Units 3810 and 3842 both have the later-style lift-off hinges and no stiffener. This was duplicated by removing the hinges and carefully shaving off the stiff-

ener (save it for later). The new hinges were made from lengths of Grandt Line .020 dia. rod. The Athearn battery-box doors are "bolted on," with two louvers near the top. Unit 3810 has a similar door except it has a stiffener rib about midway up...guess where it comes from.

The doors on 3842 are quite different: lift off hinges, two latches, four small louvers in two pairs and a stiffener rib across the top. The hinges were made the same way from Grandt rod; the stiffener is a piece of beveled .010 x .020 styrene; the latches were cut from Cannon doors and sanded thin. The louvers were made with a narrowed #16 X-Acto® chisel blade. (The Cannon sub bases make this a whole lot easier since they provide all the proper door combinations.) Some Grandt .010 dia. rod was cut into

The rear of 3810 (left) and 3842 (right) before painting clearly shows the modifications made to each unit. Compare the differences between the anti-climbers; 3810's is smooth while 3842's has a lip.

Bill of Materials

Manufacturer Part No.	Description
Detail Associates	
1003	Headlight
1013	Ditch lights
1024	Headlight
1104	Lift tabs
1202	Bell
1507	MU receptacles
1508	MU hose
1803	Antenna
1902	Air vents
2202	Grabirons
2206	Lift ring
2211	Coupler lift bar
2304	Wind deflectors
2505	.015 brass wire
2507	.022 brass wire
2508	.028 brass wire
2509	.033 brass wire
2713	FM radiator screen
3102	Fuel fillers
3201	15″ air reservoir
6206	Air hose
102213	Lift-bar bracket
Details West	
139	Air filter
155	Snowplow
158	Air conditioner
159	Air conditioner
161	Electrical cabinet
189	Anti-climber
196	Spare knuckle
197	Fuel-tank brackets
204	Air tank
214	Antenna
220	MU cable
224	Traction-motor cables
225	Salem air filter — Sm
226	Salem air filter — Lg
228	Ditch light
Cannon and Co.	
1009	Door set & plate
1102	Toilet hatch
1104	88″ low short hood
1202	Dash 2 sub-base
1501	Dash 2 cab
1601	Blower housing
Precision Scale	
3966	Fan housing
39036	Fuel-pressure gauge
39047	Sunshade
39097	Fuel filler
Smokey Valley	
20	GP50 handrail set
104A	Handrail stanchion
104B	Handrail stanchion
Microscale	
87-369	Santa Fe diesel
87-527	Diesel data
87-619	Santa Fe (EMD style)
Overland	
9676	Speed recorder
Athearn	
4626	GP50 w/dynamics (undec)
46638	GP50 dynamic-brake housing
Proto Power/A-Line	
29200	Windshield wipers
29210	Diesel Sunshades
29237	GP50 steps
70321	Mashima motor w/flywheels
Accu+paint	
1	White
2	Black
4	BAR Blue
40	Aluminum
64	ATSF Yellow
67	UP Armor Yellow
101	Satin
102	Semi-Gloss
Gunze Sangyo	
	Mr. Surfacer 1000
	Mr. Thinner
Builders in Scale	
250	40 lpi blackened chain
Throttle Up	
SL050	Synthetic load
PBL	
111	Grabiron end
Kadee	
5	Coupler
MV Lenses	
LS20	Lens set
LS22	Lens set
Jay Bee	
102	40″ nickel-silver wheels
Floquil	
Misc.	Black, Grimy Black, Roof Brown, Rust, Gray
Miniatures By Eric	
H-15	Horn
Grandt Line	
3901	.010 styrene rod
3902	.020 styrene rod
K&S Engineering	
149	.062 square brass tube
Evergreen Scale Models	
100	.010 x .020
101	.010 x .030
106	.010 x .125
107	.010 x .156
108	.010 x .188
111	.015 x .030
113	.015 x .060
116	.015 x .125
120	.020 x .020
122	.020 x .040
124	.020 x .080
125	.020 x .100
131	.030 x .030
136	.030 x .125
158	.060 x .188
176	.100 x .125
9009	.005 sheet
9010	.010 sheet
9015	.015 sheet
9020	.020 sheet

pieces about .060 long and glued into the groove between the traction-motor duct and the deck surface to represent the weld beads used in the construction. Since the welds are not uniformly spaced, locate them about .06/.08 apart.

The cab, nose and sub base can be glued in place now. Add a Cannon toilet hatch to the top of the nose of 3842 along with the Cannon angled blower housing. The high headlight casting on 3810 is DA1024, which is applied to the Cannon numberboard box after the blanking plate is sanded off.

I belong to the La Mesa Club in San Diego and transport my engines down there to run them over the Tehachapi Pass layout; to avoid handling damage I have always used brass sunshades for their robustness. Originally the cast-brass Precision Scale (PSC) 39047 parts were used since they mount by means of two substantial pins, however I have switched to A-line's 29210 etched-brass sunshades which are thinner and adjustable. Pieces of the Cannon sunshade track are cut and fit to hide the mounting hole.

The Athearn dynamic-brake casting is modified by removing the fan housing and replacing it with see-through PSC3966 which is normally a radiator fan housing, but the Santa Fe units definitely have a taller housing than the PSC dynamic-fan housing or the solid Athearn housing provides.

The other modification to the dynamic casting — revising the exhaust housing — is for 3842 only. On the Phase II units the exhaust outlet is farther forward on the housing. As molded it is .020 from the rear edge and needs to be .120 from the front edge. I accomplished this by first completely removing the existing exhaust housing. Then using a spare Athearn 46638 dynamic-brake casting, the exhaust housing was cut out and the base sanded down. Before it is installed the stack must be moved .100. This was done by cutting out the exhaust with a razor then enlarging the opening .100 to the rear. A piece of .100 wide styrene is added at the front of the hole and blended smooth before the exhaust is replaced. Two deflectors of .015 x .060 x .160 are added to each side of the stack.

On 3810 the panels in front of and behind the fan housing were removed and replaced with "X" panels made from diagonally scored and creased .005 x .155 x .620 styrene as described in the NS C39-8 article in the September 1993 issue of *Railroad Model Craftsman* that Ed Ryan and I did. Add the DA lift rings and install the dynamic housing to the shell.

Next month, we'll finish detailing the body and underframe and discuss painting and weathering.

The technique for forming battery-box louvers using a modified chisel blade is shown on 3842.

The front of 3842 after modifications but before painting.

Phase II 3842 sits nose to nose with sister Phase I 3810.

(Part I appeared in the January 1995 issue.)

The roofs of Santa Fe engines contain many extra details, so let's add them now. The air conditioner on 3810 is a DW158 Vapor type, while 3842 has a modified DW159 Prime type. I replaced the round screen with a .160 square of screen from DA2713 FM radiator screens. The air conditioners are mounted .150 back from the flat front of the cab and centered.

Both engines have antenna platforms for the EOT device mounted on the right side of the cab roof .040 from the back edge. The platform is .010 x .188 x .250 with sides of .010 x .125 x .250 and has a DW214 small Sinclair antenna mounted in the center. You could use the platform that comes with the antenna if you like it; I don't. The radio-antenna platform on 3810 is .020 x .415 x .570 styrene with the top edge radiused to represent bent sheet metal. It mounts on the left side at the rear of the inertial air filter housing on legs of .030 x .030 x .080 high on the outside with the right side legs shortened to fit the filter housing. It also has a .100 x .100 notch in the rear to allow access to the lift ring on the filter housing. The antenna platform on 3842 is .010 x .350 x .350 with the corners chamfered .020 x .020 and sitting on legs of .030 x .030 x .130; it is located flush with the rear of the cab and the left edge is even with the left edge of the flat portion of the roof. Both radio platforms have the DA1803 large Sinclair antennas, centered. Conduit made from .030 dia. brass wire is formed and runs from the top of the numberboard box to under each platform; it is secured with opened-up DA2206 lift rings.

These three photos show close-ups of the roof detail on 3819, a Phase I unit.

This look-down view
of the engineer's side of 3842
provides a good view of the roof detail.

These two photos show the roof of 3842, a Phase II locomotive.

A beacon mounting bracket is applied to 3810 on the left side, made from .010 x .188 x .188 with one side .010 x .030 x .188 and the other side taller (.010 x .156 x .188) to compensate for the roof slope.

Unit 3810 has the horn mounted in the original position above the headlight. I used brass H-15 horns from Miniatures by Eric for both units, with 3810's mounted on a .060 long piece of K&S .062 square brass tubing laid on its side and soldered together with a pin extending from the bottom for mounting. The horn on 3842 has been moved back to the left rear of the dynamic-brake housing, .100 from the rear and .150 from the side. The mounting bracket is an "A" frame made from .010 x .060 brass strip, bent and soldered to the horn. A .015 dia. air line runs from the original mounting location around the air conditioner back to the rear horn mount. Use three DA2206 lift rings to secure it to the roof. The final antenna platforms are for the Locotrol and are .010 x .156 x .156 mounted on trapezoidal end plates .010 x .090 high x .156 wide at the top tapering to .080 wide at the bottom. The platforms are mounted at the edge of the long hood, centered between the last two radiator fans. Mount DW214 small Sinclair antennas with the right side one facing forward and the left one facing backwards.

A DA2208 V-shaped grabiron is located behind the rear fan. The conduit to the motors in the Q fans is made with .028 dia. brass wire bent about 90° and running from the pad Athearn provides to the side of the

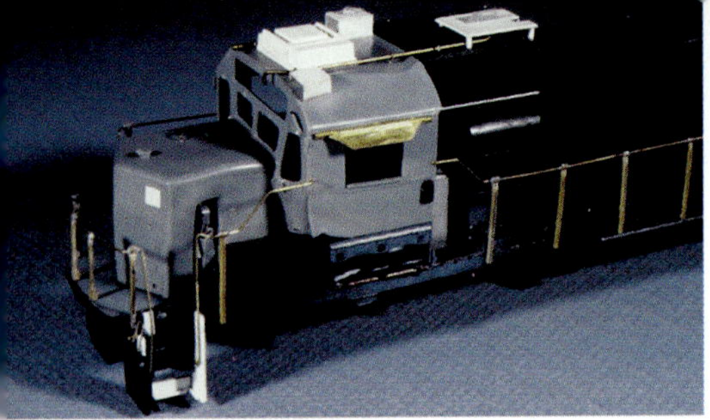

This is what happens when photo-floods are brought in too close and kept on too long. The cab and short hood, and all the companion detail, on 3810 had to be cut off and redone.

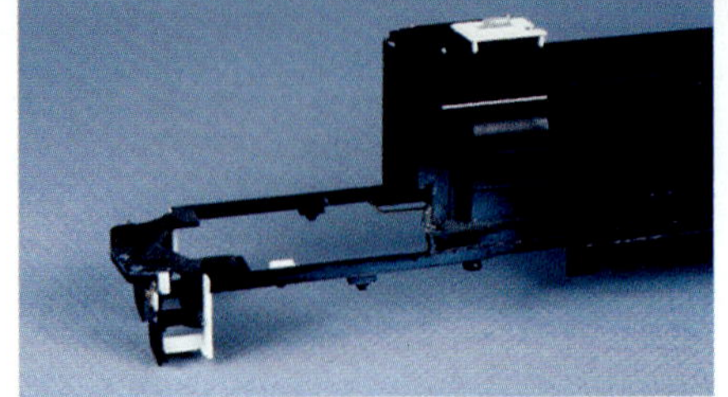

The cab, sub-base and nose have been removed.

The accident did have a positive result since it forced me to redo the sub-base with Cannon parts.

fan housing. There is one each per fan, and they are not all located the same. Drill a hole in each of the three fan lifting lugs. Remove the sand-filler hatch and replace with the extra one provided in the Cannon nose kit. As long as we're at the rear of the long hood, let's make one improvement to the lift tabs on the radiator grilles. Take a sharp razor and cut behind them against the hood and with the blade bend them out slightly.

The inertial filter screens on each side of the hood behind the cab need a strip of .015 x .030 styrene added to the lower side of the fan housing.

screen similar to the top. Remove the electrical cabinet door on the right side behind the cab by shaving and sanding and replace with the Cannon "floating" door from set HD-1009. A DW161 electrical cabinet filter was applied behind the cab on 3810.

As I mentioned, the step wells were modified to produce the "notch" effect on the side of the step well away from the pilot. The process is somewhat involved and will be the subject of another article. The steps were removed and replaced with see-through versions cut to size from the etched material from the DA2713 Fairbanks Morse radiator screens; a lip was formed and bent down from the border material. A-line has announced etched steps for the Athearn GP38/40/50 shells that should work for

these. It was at this juncture that I was taking model photos of the steps on 3810 and got the front end too close to the lights and damaged the cab and nose with the heat. After recording the evidence (not my language) I sawed the entire cab/nose/Athearn sub-base off. I was able to salvage the roof details to reuse. Finally I was able to use the entire Cannon cab/nose/sub-base assembly after all, although I don't recommend this method.

Detail Under the Walkway

Under the walkways we still have more work to do. Since I removed the stock air reservoirs, new ones must be made to replace them. I used the DA3201 plastic reservoirs but cut and sanded off all the brackets that are supplied for roof mounting. They were attached under the walk after first grinding away part of the shell thickness to allow them to mount closer to the edge of the shell and clear the fuel tank. I added the relief valves that come with the DW204 reservoir. Before attaching the reservoir, drill a hole in each end to clear the .022 dia. brass wire that is used for air-line plumbing.

The lines that come out the rear of each tank go straight a short ways then bend up and disappear from sight. The front left pipe "tees" almost immediately before bending back on itself behind the tank with the branch going up and out of sight. The "tees" or any other pipe fitting are made by applying a drop of thick CA with a piece of wire to the pipe then hitting it with the Kicker. More CA is applied if necessary to produce a blob which represents a fitting. The "tees" are soldered together first.

The plumbing on the right gets more complicated due to the air filters. Unit 3810 uses the DW139 set; follow the instructions for the plumbing. Unit 3842 uses the newer DW225 small Salem filters. Both units have the DW226 large Salem air dryer mounted under the left walkway, adjacent to the rear step well.

DA1507 or DW220 MU receptacles can be added under the anti-climber a little to the right of center. A piece of .015 x .125 x 1.05 is glued across the bottom of the rear pilot, and a pair of straight grabirons is added on each side to keep the MU hoses from flopping around. Adding the DA2211 cut bars mounted in DA102213 brass brackets (for robustness) to each pilot completes most of the work to the shell prior to painting (except the handrails).

Fireman's side of 3810 before painting clearly shows details that were added to this Phase I unit.

Compare this photo of 3842 before painting to that of 3810 and you can see the specific details that distinguish this Phase II GP50 from the Phase I.

Engineer's side of cab area on 3810 before painting.

Engineer's side of cab on 3842 before painting.

Fireman's side of cab on 3842.

I prefer to use the Smokcy Valley cast-brass handrail stanchions with my own bent .015 dia. brass-wire railings. SV20 for the GP50 is a good start, with some additional SV stanchions. The long side handrails are formed up and soldered to the stanchions one at a time right on the model...all you need is five hands to keep everything in place and still hold the soldering iron. To make this easier, I place all the stanchions in the holes and apply a piece of drafting tape along the walkway to keep them from falling out or over. The wire is pre-bent to the proper step-well configuration except for the last bend where it attaches to the step. The handrail is then located in the notches of the stanchions and held in place with a scrap of foam that has been cut in a taper. The foam piece is wedged in place behind the handrail and the shell and located between the first couple stanchions. I then apply Tix Flux to the first joint and touch it quickly with a very hot (800°) pencil-tip soldering iron, tinned with a very small amount of solder on the tip. With the flux and a hot, tinned iron the contact time to make the joint is almost nothing, and the heat is in and out of the joint so quickly that the heat doesn't have time to travel down the stanchion and melt the plastic. Move the foam wedge as you go to keep the wire located in the stanchion notch, working from one end to the other. After the entire assembly is assembled, any stanchion straightening can be done by applying flux to the joint and using needle-nose pliers to move the stanchion while the heat is applied. Be sure to use the two tall stanchions for either side of the angled blower duct on 3842.

For the front and rear stanchions to be correct for the prototype some changes are made. First on 3810 all the rear stanchions mount on the top of the deck not the side, so plug and fill the stock holes with styrene rod. New holes are drilled in the top of the deck .150 each side of center to accept SV104B stanchions in the center locations; the outer ones are SV104A and are located .410 from center. Before mounting the front stanchions on 3810, I added some scraps of styrene under the DW anti-climber since it is very thin and the stanchion holes work loose and allow the handrails to move around. The center stanchions are the same SV104B as used on the back. The outer stanchions mount to the side of the anti-climber

just in front of the pilot. I used the short side stanchions for these.

For 3842 both ends are the same with SV104B at the center and SV104A for the outside location. All are mounted on the top of the deck at the .150 and .410 dimensions from center. Bend the end handrails per the photos. After all the soldering is done mark the location for the final bend into the shell, remove the assemblies, make the bend and check fit again. Then drill the attaching holes for the ends and glue a PBL111 NBW next to the hole. Remove the assemblies again and give them a good washing with dish soap and a tooth brush to remove the flux since it is corrosive. Add the SV bolt plates and the box section doublers to the side end stanchions. One more thing I do is drill a .016 hole in all the center stanchions at the flat area just below the handrail to accommodate a DA2206 lift ring and chain which is installed after painting. Also CA a piece of .015 dia. wire into the channel of the center stanchions to represent the break-away mount for the chains.

The Underframe

When I started this I wasn't thinking ahead, and I used the stock Athearn chassis instead of the pre-leaded Proto Power West version, which makes installing the can motor easier. Since I do so many modifications to the frame I find it is better to buy the separate parts and build my own PPW compatible

drive. I modify all my Athearn Geeps to reduce the gap between the top of the trucks and the bottom of the frame and lower the ride height. This is done by spot facing down the truck contact surface .025 with a special ⁵⁄₈" dia. end mill with a .093 dia. hole in the center of it. At the same time the end surfaces of the fuel tank are squared up to remove the mold draft. This can be done with a file or an end mill. The Athearn parting-line flash down the side of the fuel tank is filed and sanded smooth, and the lumps representing the fuel filler are removed.

The process to reduce the gap is done in two steps: lower the chassis .025 by spot facing, and add .015 styrene to the bottom surface of the frame portion of the chassis to simulate the I-beam construction. This effectively reduces the gap by .040. Before adding the styrene, part of the extra material along the frame sides is cut away, leaving only the bolsters intact. Refer to the photos since it is difficult to describe what is removed.

I also removed enough material from the top of the coupler mounts so that a Kadee® No. 5 coupler mounted in its box will sit at the correct height when sitting on top of the chassis. The Kadee box is assembled after removing the side ears, top lip and some excess material from the rear. Also add a .010 shim to the bottom inside of the box to keep the coupler from drooping. After the box is glued together, tap the hole with a 4-40 tap. I also remove the "glad hand" from

CANADIAN PACIFIC GP35

by Patrick Lawson

Photos by the author

CANADIAN PACIFIC modelers get a break when it comes to modeling the GP35. Kato has produced a superb-running, beautifully detailed model of a Phase 1a GP35 in the classic tuscan-and-gray paint scheme of the prototype. *(Editor's Note: Kato's Phase 1b GP35 in the red "Pac-Man" scheme with narrow stripes on hood ends and cab front and small multimark should be available later this month.)* They have done an excellent job of applying the paint. It is up to the modeler, with only a small amount of effort, to produce a model that faithfully follows the prototype. Those of you that have modeled one or more of the legions of CP Rail SD40-2s, none of which are identical or easy to model, will find the CP Rail GP35s are a welcome relief.

CP Rail's roster of 23 GP35 units is relatively small. Twenty four of them were purchased from 1964 through 1966. Unit number 5018 was retired in 1974. All of the units were de-rated from 2,500-hp to 2,250, possibly to make them compatible with the two GP30 units CP already had. Units numbered 5014-5025 were rebuilt from traded-in FP7A, F7B, F9B and GP7 units. In 1965, units numbered 8202-8213 were renumbered 5002-5013.

A builder's photograph of unit 8204, taken at GMD, London, Ontario, in 1964,

that appears in *Rail Canada, Vol. 3* by Donald Lewis, shows the units were painted in tuscan and gray with striking yellow stripes on the front and rear pilots. The numbers on the side of the cab were in the tuscan panel, lower than usual for CP units. The side handrails and posts were tuscan, and the front handrails and posts were yellow. I mention this because just two years later, unit 5025, although in the tuscan scheme,

was painted quite differently; it is also pictured in Lewis's *Rail Canada, Vol. 3*. Gone were the front and rear yellow stripes on the pilots, and the numbers on the side of the cab were moved up to the gray panel below the window. The front handrails were still yellow, but the posts were gray.

At least five versions of the Action Red paint scheme have been applied to CP Rail GP35 units. I have no exact date, but in

CP Rail GP35 Specifics

Builder	GMD (General Motors Diesel in London, Ontario)
Engine	16-645D3A
HP	2,250 (de-rated from 2,500-hp)
CTE	47,000 (Continuos Tractive Effort)
Weight	261,000-262,000 lbs.
Top Speed	65 mph

Original Numbers	Current Numbers*	Serial No.	Built	Class	Total	Remaining
8202-8213	5002-5013	A2035-A2046	1964	DRS-22b	12	12
—	5014-5023	A2079-A2088	1965	DRS-22c	10	9†
—	5024-5025	A2123-A2124	1966	DRS-22d	2	2
					24	23

*Renumbering occurred in 1965. / †5018 was retired in 1974.

1969, CP began using the large multimark with narrow stripes. This scheme was soon replaced by the small multimark with narrow stripes. In the mid 1970s, when CP changed to wider 8″ stripes, the multimark was retained. I have seen no photographs of a GP35 with a large multimark and wide stripes, but this scheme was applied to other units. About 1987, CP units started coming out of the paint shop without the multimark, and these were followed by the most recent CPRS (CP Rail System) paint scheme with the Canadian/ American flag symbol on the sides and CP on the nose and rear of the units.

The Model

The Kato GP35 is a great starting point for this model. I received mine decorated in the old Canadian Pacific tuscan scheme. This model would lend itself well to the addition of details without removing the factory paint. A glance through the parts list will show that there isn't a lot of detail to be added, and most of it can be easily applied. Those of you that take this route may want to paint the details first and apply them with small amounts of CA applied from the inside of the shell whenever possible.

As nice as the tuscan model looked, I had little hesitation in placing the shell in the kitchen sink and spraying it with oven cleaner to remove the paint. The thought of removing that beautiful tuscan-and-gray paint may cause cringing and clenching of teeth in some quarters. Since this is the best model of a GP35 available, and I was modeling CP Rail in 1990, I wanted a modern unit painted in CP Action Red so I removed the factory paint.

To my eyes, no matter which paint scheme you choose, the paint simply can't hide the lack of detail that would make this model *look* like a Canadian Pacific unit. By this I mean that it is easy to marvel at the beautifully crafted fans and crisp details on the shell, but without those distinctive Canadian Pacific details such as the low-hood bell, pilot and ditch lights, it is just another GP35. In fact, some modelers may decide that the addition of only those details is "good enough."

I generally start by removing detail, so the first to go were the finely crafted footboards and one of the fans. Kato did a beautiful job of tooling these details, but what is the point of having them on a model if the prototype doesn't?

I then used methylene chloride (or plastic cement) to glue plastic sprue in the front and rear lights. When the glue had dried completely, I filed and sanded the lights to a smooth surface. While on the subject of lights, CP GP35s are one of the few CP units that have classification lights on the low nose. Most have them above the front number boards.

Installing the Miniatures by Eric Canadian steps requires the most cutting. At first glance, their installation may appear to be quite complex, but changing them is really quite straightforward. Once you have done the first one, the rest are easy. My advice is to cut out the shell's steps a bit small and file down until a good fit is achieved. I use a circular saw chucked in a Dremel tool to quickly rough them out.

There are a lot of holes that need to be drilled for the lights, eyebolts, grabirons, low-hood bell, sand hatches, horn, air hoses, coupler lift bars and antenna. To simplify construction, I drill all the necessary holes in one shot while I have my Dremel out. When

Bill of Materials

Manufacturer
Part No.   Description

Kato
  8205   Canadian Pacific GP35
Miniatures by Eric
  A5   Axle wheel indicator
  B2   Low-hood bell
  H6   Sand hatches
  H12   Winterization hatch
  H15   Air horn
  L1   Ditch lights
  L7   Double front headlight
  L51   Double rear headlights
  P5   Diesel pilot
  S17   Canadian steps
Detail Associates
  1508   Air hoses
  1803   Sinclair radio antenna
  2202   Grabirons
  2205   Coupler lift bars
  2206   Eyebolts
  2304   Cab wind deflectors
Kadee®
  5   Couplers
MV Products
  LS18   Headlight lenses
  LS22   Classification lenses
Floquil
  110004   Crystal Cote
  110010   Engine Black
  110015   Flat Finish
  Misc.   Weathering colors
Scalecoat
  11   White
  70   CP Action Red
  31   SP Daylight Red (add
        approximately one part
        per three parts CP Action
        Red to brighten red)
Herald King (decals)
  L4   CP hood unit
Accucals (decals)
  5824H   CP cab units

These photos show later-production GP35s as they appeared about 1991.

adding these details, apply CA from the inside of the shell whenever possible. I only drilled shallow pockets in the classification lights to accept MV Products jewels so I had to use caution when applying CA to these areas. I apply the CA and then pick up the jewels with a damp finger and place them in the pre-drilled sockets. The winter hatch and pilot are the details that require care when attaching. Don't apply the grabirons to the short and long hoods until the decals have been applied.

Kato has simplified painting the model by making the walkways separate from the shell. The only masking necessary is the anti-glare section on the short hood. Weather the unit carefully to reflect a prototype unit. My question on weathering is, "How many photographs do you have of fresh-from-the-paintshop units?" An examination of the prototype photos that accompany this article not only shows road grime, but also extensive fading of the red on many units.

I had some problem with paint chipping on the delrin handrails. There were three options that can be used to remedy this situation. First would be to cut the handrails from the stanchions and drill them to receive fine wire ones. The second would be to use Badger's Accu-flex paint which sticks to almost anything. And the third would be to use the new Smokey Valley GP35 handrail set (#214) which was recently released, sometime after I'd finished the model.

This is a relatively easy detailing project that results in an accurate, good-running model. ▮

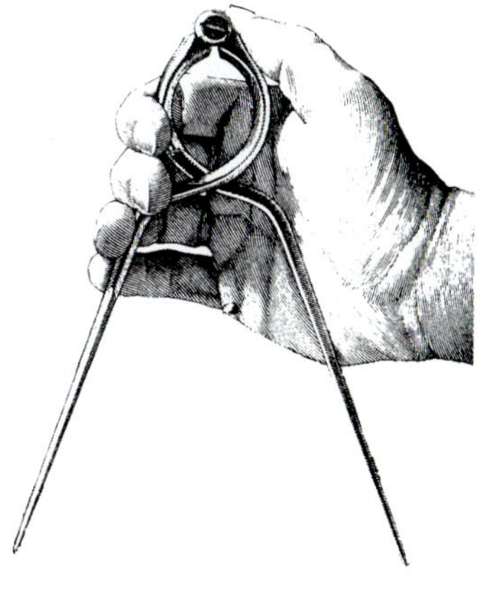

General Motors Diesel, Ltd. (GMD) Canadian National (CN) GP40-2L

HO Scale Model by Athearn
N Scale Model by Kato

by Rich Picariello

Photos from the author's collection

The Prototype GP40-2L: Production of the GP40-2 began in 1972 and ended in 1986. EMD built 812 3,000-hp GP40-2 locomotives for the U.S. and 44 for Mexico. General Motors Diesel, Ltd., EMD's Canadian subsidiary, built 275 of this model in Canada. The Canadian National acquired 267 of the total Canadian production from 1974 to 1976. The number series for these units is 9400 to 9667. All CN units were delivered with the Canadian Safety Cab. The GP40-2L (the CN classed them as GF-430c) rides on two Blomberg "M"-type four-wheel trucks.

The Scale Model GP40-2L: Athearn's HO scale GP40-2 makes an excellent starting point for this project; purchase the undecorated non-dynamic-brake version. Remove the cab, cab sub base and the short hood; the safety cab (kit) will completely replace the removed parts. CN GP40-2L units have vertical stairwells with four steps instead of the standard inclined three-step stairwells found on other prototype GP40-2 locomotives (the Athearn and Kato models have three steps); these modified steps will have to be scratchbuilt from styrene as no commercial parts are known to be available. The front and rear platform end handrails cannot be used as is; form .015 brass wire to the shape shown in the photos. The DA Canadian safety cab kit contains sand fillers (two styles), handrail wire for the front of the cab and a cab-mounted bell.

For N scale, Kato's limited-production GP40-2 may be available at some hobby dealers, flea markets or swap meets. An N scale Canadian safety cab is not known to be available so this part would have to be scratchbuilt.

Paint and Decal Notes: CN GP40-2L diesels are painted in red, white and black. Handrails are black with white at the step areas. The fuel tank, underframe, cab roof, anti-glare panel, walkways, pilots and trucks are black; the sidesill is yellow. The plow appears to be black with diagonal white stripes. Microscale makes a separate stripe set for those who do not wish to mask and paint the diagonal long-hood stripes. Both Floquil and Accupaint have CN red paint in their lines; attempting to accurately match CN red in Scalecoat and Accu-flex paints will require mixing colors in order to obtain the proper shade.

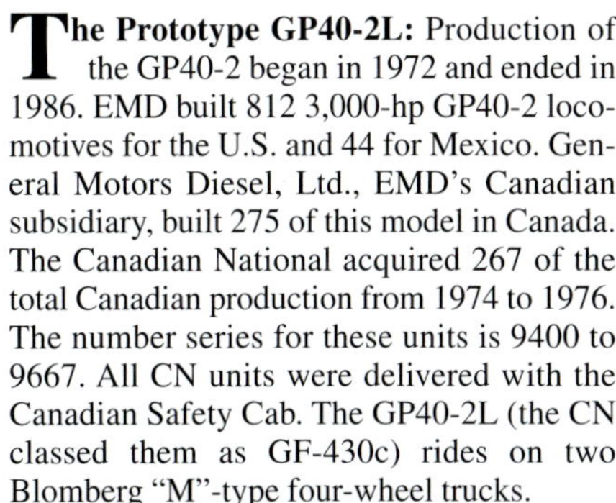

Canadian National GP40-2L

Detail Parts for HO Scale:

#	Part	Description	Price
1 -	DW139	Air filter	1.00/2
2 -	DA1601	Air horn (delrin)	1.75/2
	OM9014	Air horn (brass)	3.50/ea.
3 -	DA3201	Air tanks (plastic)*	2.25/2
	DW204	Air tanks (metal)*	1.95/2
4 -	CF201	Antenna, Sinclair (brass)	3.79/4
	DA1803	Antenna, Sinclair (plastic)	1.25/4
5 -	DW189	Anticlimber	1.25/ea.
6 -	CF230	Bell (brass)	3.09/ea.
7 -	DW177	Brake wheel w/gear box	1.50/ea.
8 -	DW195	Buffer plate, pilots (optional)	1.50/2
9 -	DA3604	Canadian Safety Cab kit	10.95/ea.
10 -	PSC48348	Chain	2.75/10"
11 -	MV502	Classification lenses (red, green & amber)*	1.00/3

Note: Need two sets; drill out the molded-on class lights to mount the MV lenses.

#	Part	Description	Price
12 -	DA2205	Coupler lift bar	2.75/10
	OM9150	Coupler lift bar	1.70/2
13 -	OM9171	Door handle (brass)	3.35/6
	PSC3998	Door handle (plastic)	1.50/6
14 -	DA1404	Drop step	1.50/2

Note: One step needed, mounted on rear deck only.

#	Part	Description	Price
15 -	PSC3978	Exhaust stack*	1.50/ea.
16 -	DA2006	Fan w/blades (plastic)*	7.95/3
	DW144	Fan (plastic)*	1.25/3
	OM9216	Fan w/blades (brass — need three)*	3.85/ea.
	PSC3932	Fan (plastic)*	2.25/4
17 -	DA3102	Fuel filler (plastic)†	1.00/set
	DW166	Fuel filler (metal)	1.00/4
	PSC39080	Fuel filler (plastic)	1.50/4
18 -	DA3101	Fuel gauge	1.00/6

Note: Needed on right side of fuel tank only.

#	Part	Description	Price
19 -	DA3102	Fuel sight glass (plastic)†	1.00/set
	CF226	Fuel sight glass (brass)	2.09/2
	OM9250	Fuel sight glass (brass)	3.00/ea.
	PSC39011	Fuel sight glass (plastic)	1.50/2
20 -	DA2202	Grabirons	2.50/48
	UP54	Grabirons (brass)	5.95/12
21 -	DA2217	Grabirons, curved	1.50/3
22 -	DA2215	Grabirons, ladder notched	2.00/12
23 -	SV30	Handrails (optional)	15.95/set
24 -	DA1004	Headlight, front*	1.00/2
25 -	DA1014	Headlight, rear, single lens (plastic)	1.00/2

Note: Cut and/or file off the double light on the long hood.

#	Part	Description	Price
26 -	MV22	Headlight lenses	1.10/4
27 -	DA6206	Hose, air line	1.25/6
28 -	CC1301	Inertial filter*	1.95/4
29 -	DA2206	Lift rings	3.00/36
30 -	DA1104	Lift tabs	.85/16
31 -	CA424	Louvers (stamped aluminum)	1.50/24
	DA1905	Louvers (plastic)	3.95/48
32 -	DA1505	MU stand	1.25/2
33 -	CF257	MU hoses, 3-per bracket (brass)	4.95/4
	DA1508	MU hoses (delrin)	2.00/16
	OM9350	MU hoses, 3-per bracket (brass)	6.05/4
34 -	DW155	Plow pilot	1.50/ea.
35 -	CC1404	Radiator screens*	3.95/4
36 -	DW119	Rerailer w/hangers	1.50/2
37 -	DA3001	Sand-fill hatch (plastic)*	1.25/6
	OM9400	Sand-fill hatch (brass)*	3.30/2
38 -	AL29210	Sunshade (photo-etched brass)	1.95/6
	DA1301	Sunshade (plastic)	1.25/6
	DW188	Sunshade (plastic)	.80/4
	PSC39047	Sunshade (brass)	2.25/4
39 -	CF112	Underframe/step light (brass)	2.95/2
	DW172	Underframe/step light	1.25/8
40 -	CF195	Wheel-slip modulator	4.39/4
41 -	DA2304	Wind deflector	2.50/set
	UP77	Wind deflector/mirror	2.00/2
42 -	AL29200	Windshield wipers (delrin)	1.75/8
	CS419	Windshield wipers (brass)	3.50/4
	PSC3968	Windshield wipers (plastic)	1.50/4
	UP94	Windshield wipers (brass)	2.00/4
	UP97	Windshield wipers (plastic)	1.50/4

* Similar parts, either separate or molded on, are included with the Athearn scale model and/or the (DA) Canadian Safety Cab kit; replacement of any or all original parts is left to the discretion of the modeler.

† DA3102 Fuel Tank Fittings (set) contains other parts that may or may not be needed for this detailing project.

Note: The following parts must be fabricated by the modeler: **A** — Anticlimber brace — make from thin styrene. **B** — Modified jacking pads — fabricate from styrene. **C** — Brake cylinder air line — form from brass wire. **D** — Vertical steps — make from styrene (need four). **E** — Walkway blower guard — make from styrene.

AL/ PPW: A-Line/Proto Power West
P.O. Box 7916
La Verne, CA 91750

CS: Cal-Scale
21 Howard Street
Montoursville, PA 17754

CC: Cannon and Company
310 Willow Heights
Aptos, CA 95003

CA: Cary Locomotive Works
21 Howard Street
Montoursville, PA 17754

CF: Custom Finishing
379 Tully Road
Orange, MA 01364

DA: Detail Associates
Box 5357
San Luis Obispo, CA 93403

DW: Details West
P.O. Box 5132
Hacienda Heights, CA 91745

MV: MV Products
P.O. Box 6622
Orange, CA 92667

OM: Overland Models Inc.
5908 W. Kilgore Avenue.
Muncie, IN 47304

PSC: Precision Scale Company
3961 Hwy. 93 North
Stevensville, MT 59870

SV: Smokey Valley Railroad Products
P.O. Box 32
Dublin, OH 43017

UP: Utah Pacific
Div. of Tomar Industries
9520 E. Napier Avenue
Benton Harbor, MI 49022

Note: These detail parts may be available at your local hobby dealer(s), so try there first. If you must order directly from a manufacturer, include at least **$3.50** for postage and handling. You must purchase the full quantities as shown in the detail parts list.

DECALS:

HO Scale:
C-D-S 212 (dry transfers)
Herald King L-161
Microscale 87-567 (CN lettering set)
Microscale 87-568 (CN diesel stripes)

N Scale:
Microscale 60-567 (CN lettering set)
Microscale 60-568 (CN diesel stripes)

PAINTS:

Accu-flex:
16-01 Engine Black
16-02 Reefer White
16-10 Reefer Yellow
16-58 Amtrak Red (close)

Accupaint:
1 Stencil White
2 Stencil Black
18 CN Red-Orange
20 Medium Yellow

Floquil:
110010 Engine Black
110011 Reefer White
110031 Reefer Yellow
110250 CN Orange #11

Scalecoat:
10 Black
11 White
15 Reefer Yellow
31 SP Daylight Red (close)

General Electric Company (GE)
Chicago and Northwestern (CNW) C40-8
HO and N Scale Models by Bachmann Spectrum

by Rich Picariello

Photos by the author

The Prototype C40-8: GE introduced their 4,000-hp Dash 8-40C in late 1987. This locomotive has an overall length of 70′ 8″ and truck centers of 43′ 4″; they ride on two GE six-wheel trucks.

The CNW took delivery of their 77 Dash 8-40C locomotives (CNW classifies them as C40-8) from 1989 to 1991; they are numbered from 8501 to 8577. Number 8542 is decorated with a special Wyoming Centennial logo (see photo).

The Scale Model C40-8: Bachmann's HO scale Spectrum Dash 8-40C locomotive is available decorated for the CNW with two road numbers. The Spectrum models have more detail and run better than the regular series of Bachmann diesel locomotives. On the Bachmann Dash 8-40C, the truck sideframes have the axle snubber and the brake cylinders molded-on; the sideframes can be replaced with the listed DA sideframes; this will greatly improve the appearance of the trucks.

Bachmann also offers the Dash 8-40C in N scale, decorated for the CNW.

Paint and Decal Notes: Bachmann's HO and N scale Dash 8-40Cs are available decorated for the CNW and are fairly well done except for the overly thick paint. Some modelers may wish to start with an undecorated model and paint and decal it themselves. CNW units are painted in yellow and dark green. The yellow used is referred to as "Zeto" Yellow which is noticeably lighter then the old CNW Yellow used previously. Due to fading problems with this paint, most units have been repainted with a darker yellow that is close to the old CNW yellow. Only Accu-flex has both of the CNW yellows in their line; both Floquil and Scalecoat CNW (old) yellows can be lightened with white to more closely match Zeto Yellow. Handrails are green with white trim at the step areas. The underframe, trucks and the fuel tank are black; step edges are white. GE builders plates are available on Microscale set MC-4056 (HO scale only).

DIE
CLO
Ro
8515
C40-8
8515
CHICAGO NORTH WESTERN SYSTEM
33
C
B
31
12
13
12
14
29
31
A
8
4
3
32
30
22
21
22
21
2
11
8567
8567
9322
10
11
9
31
A
5
12
14
13
12
31
22
33
32
33
B
8548
17
19
11
8548
C40-8
6
7
T
he
petitive
produc
of the 2
the maj
distant
in 1966
duction
follow-
phase I
1
9
7
15
25
23
1
9
7
15
25
23
20
24
23

decorated for the Rock Island. Use the Stewart phase IV U25B to model the phase I U28B. Rock Island UBs did not have dynamic brakes; remove the dynamic-brake resistors in the grille openings on the Stewart shell.

The Atlas U25B can be used in N scale; Atlas diesel locomotives are limited-production models with only periodic availability. Start with an undecorated model and add the appropriate N scale detail parts and decals.

Paint and Decal Notes: Rock Island had more diesel paint schemes and lettering variations over the years than perhaps any other railroad. One of the last schemes in use before the final light blue "The Rock" scheme was the maroon carbody with a yellow low nose. On the U25B/U28B, the fuel tank could be painted either maroon or black; the trucks were black, the handrail stanchions were maroon and the handrails were aluminum with white at the step areas. The Rock Island

roadname once appeared on the long hood but was eliminated on many units in later years. A white stripe runs along the length of the sidesills. Only Floquil had a Rock Island Maroon paint in their line, but it has been discontinued; some hobby shops may still have some in stock. The other listed maroons may have to be lightened or darkened to more closely match the photos. These units display moderate to severe weathering, especially in the final years of the Rock Island.

Rock Island U25B

Detail Parts for HO Scale:

#	Part	Description	Price
1 -	DW139	Air filter	1.00/2
2 -	CS421	Air horn (brass)	6.95/ea.
	DA1602	Air horn (delrin)	1.75/2
	OM9005	Air horn (brass)	3.20/ea.
	Note: On Nos. 219 and 223.		
3 -	CS425	Air horn (brass)	4.95/ea.
	DA1601	Air horn (delrin)	1.75/2
	DW175	Air horn (brass)	2.50/ea.
	Note: On #244 only.		
4 -	CF113	Antenna	3.09/2
	DW157	Antenna	1.50/6
5 -	DA2302	Armrest, cab	1.25/8
6 -	DA1202	Bell, underframe	1.00/2
	DW127	Bell, underframe	1.25/2
7 -	DW132	Brake ratchet	1.00/ea.
	Note: On #244 only.		
8 -	DW179	Brake wheel	1.00/2
	Note: On #219 only.		
9 -	PSC48348	Chain	2.75/10"
10 -	MV22	Classification lenses	1.15/4
11 -	DA2205	Coupler lift bar	2.75/10
	OM9150	Coupler lift bar	1.70/2
12 -	PSC3998	Door handle (plastic)	1.50/6
	OM9171	Door handle (brass)	1.65/2
13 -	DA1403	Drop step	1.25/2
14 -	UP69	Exhaust stack (brass)*	2.50/ea.
15 -	DW149	Fuel filler, GE	1.00/4
16 -	OM9252	Fuel sight glass	1.70/ea.
17 -	DA2202	Grabirons	2.50/48
18 -	PL181	Grille, Farr (etched stainless steel)	2.75/2
	Note: U25B numbers 225 and up were delivered with this grille; also used on early U28Bs.		
19 -	MV280	Headlight lenses	1.50/4
20 -	CS277	Hose, air line (brass)	2.15/4
	DA6206	Hose, air line (delrin)	1.25/6
21 -	DA1108	Lift rings, GE (plastic)*	1.50/12
	UP62	Lift rings, GE (brass)*	2.00/10
22 -	CF257	MU hoses, 3-per bracket (brass)	4.95/4
	DA1508	MU hoses, individual (delrin)	2.00/16
	OM9350	MU hoses, 3-per bracket (brass)	6.10/4
23 -	DA1507	MU receptacles & covers	1.25/30
24 -	DW155	Plow pilot	1.50/ea.
25 -	DA3001	Sand-fill hatch	1.25/6
26 -	CF196	Speed recorder (brass)	4.39/4
	DA2807	Speed recorder (delrin)	1.50/4
27 -	AL29210	Sunshade, cab (etched brass)	1.95/6
	DA1301	Sunshade, cab (plastic)	1.25/6
	DW188	Sunshade, cab (plastic)	.80/4
	PSC39047	Sunshade, cab (brass)	2.25/4
28 -	CF112	Underframe/step light (brass)	2.95/2
	DW172	Underframe/step light (metal)	1.25/8
29 -	CF195	Wheel-slip modulator	4.39/4
30 -	DA2312	Wind deflector (clear plastic)	1.25/4
	UP77	Wind deflector/mirror (brass)	2.00/2
31 -	AL29200	Windshield wipers (delrin)	1.75/8
	CS419	Windshield wipers (brass)	3.50/4
	PSC3968	Windshield wipers (plastic)	1.50/4
	UP94	Windshield wipers (brass)	2.00/4
	UP97	Windshield wipers (plastic)	1.50/4

The following parts must be fabricated by the modeler:

A — Brake-cylinder air line — make from brass wire.

B — ACI label plates — make from .005 styrene or brass, add ACI decals.

C — Sunshade mounting bracket — make from small plastic angle stock.

D — Low-nose hand grabs — form from .015 brass wire.

E — Ladder — use the Stewart part or use a modified plastic HO scale freight car ladder.

* Similar parts, either separate or molded on, are included with the Stewart Hobbies HO scale model. Replacement of any or all original parts is left to the discretion of the modeler.

AL/ PPW: *A-Line/Proto Power West*
P.O. Box 7916
La Verne, CA 91750

CS: *Cal-Scale*
21 Howard Street
Montoursville, PA 17754

CF: *Custom Finishing*
379 Tully Road
Orange, MA 01364

DA: *Detail Associates*
Box 5357
San Luis Obispo, CA 93403

DW: *Details West*
P.O. Box 5132
Hacienda Heights, CA 91745

MV: *MV Products*
P.O. Box 6622
Orange, CA 92667

OM: *Overland Models Inc.*
5908 W. Kilgore Avenue.
Muncie, IN 47304

PL: *Plano Model Products*
2701 W. 15th Street
Suite 113
Plano, TX 75075

PSC: *Precision Scale Company*
3961 Hwy. 93 North
Stevensville, MT 59870

SV: *Smokey Valley Railroad Products*
P.O. Box 339
Plantersville, MS 38862

UP: *Utah Pacific*
9520 E. Napier Avenue
Benton Harbor, MI 49022

Note: These detail parts may be available at your local hobby dealer(s), so try there first. If you must order directly from a manufacturer, include at least **$3.50** for postage and handling. You must purchase the full quantities as shown in the detail parts list.

DECALS:	**PAINTS:**		**Accu+paint:**		**Floquil:**		**Scalecoat:**	
HO Scale:	**Accu-flex:**		2	Stencil Black	110010	Engine Black	10	Black
Champion EH-198	16-01	Engine Black	9	Cornell Red	110031	Reefer Yellow	15	Reefer Yellow
Herald King L-544	16-10	Reefer Yellow		(close)	110160	Rock Island	62	LV Cornell Red
Microscale 87-18	16-15	Maroon Tuscan	20	Medium Yellow		Maroon		(close)
N Scale:		Oxide Red				(discontinued)		
Microscale 60-18		(close)						

CENTRAL OF GEORGIA SD7/9s

in CLASSIC BLUE and GRAY

by Larry Puckett

Photos by the author unless otherwise indicated

Few modelers outside the South would ever know that the Central of Georgia Railroad (CoG) even existed were it not for the "C.G." sublettering on some Norfolk Southern locomotives. However, this onetime regional carrier commands a strong following among railfans in Georgia and the Southeast, and they are particularly fond of the striking blue-and-gray paint scheme that adorned the CoG's first-generation diesels. But before we look at that paint scheme, let's first take a quick look at the railroad that it represented.

A History Lesson

The Central of Georgia Railroad was originally organized in 1833 as the Central Rail Road and Canal Company with the objective of connecting Savannah and Macon, GA. By 1843 this task had been accomplished, and over the ensuing decades the line was expanded through purchases, leases and mergers to Augusta, Athens, Atlanta and Columbus, in Georgia; Birmingham, Montgomery, Andalusia and Lockhart, in Alabama; and Chattanooga, in Tennessee. In 1895 the company was incorporated as the Central of Georgia Railway. By 1907 the Central of Georgia had become one of Edward H. Harriman's roads, which lead to ownership by the Illinois Central in 1909 — a relation that would continue beyond the end of Illinois Central control in 1932. (The *Seminole* and *City of Miami* streamliners were jointly operated by the IC and CoG until the coming of Amtrak). The Frisco attempted to purchase the controlling interests in the CoG in 1956 but failed to gain ICC approval and was forced to sell its stock in the company to the Southern Railway in 1963. In 1971 the Central of Georgia Railway (plus a few smaller affiliated roads) was merged completely into the Southern as the Central of Georgia Railroad, and in 1982 it became part of the Norfolk Southern.

Paint Schemes

During the diesel era CoG locomotives wore eight different paint schemes, some of

1 — Central of Georgia SD7 #201 waits at the yard throat for its train to be made up.

2 — After completing a local run #201 heads back to the diesel fueling rack for servicing.

them the result of the various mergers and ownership changes. Prior to World War II the CoG owned an assortment of switchers from ALCo, Baldwin, EMD and Fairbanks Morse. These were painted in a plain black scheme with white stripes along the sill and hood. Beginning with the delivery of E7s in 1946, the blue-and-gray scheme with a stylized winged herald was adopted for all locomotives until the delivery of GP18s in 1960. The early 1960s' scheme was similar to its predecessor with the exception that the stylized wings were dropped from the herald and the blue and gray were replaced with Pullman Green.

As a result of the joint operation of the *Seminole* two CoG E8s were painted into the Illinois Central orange-and-chocolate-brown scheme although retaining the "Central of Georgia" roadname. In 1963 an experimental scheme, consisting of a black unit with white lettering and stylized wing on the nose was tried on two E7s. Dubbed the "Hitler mustache" scheme, it was short-lived.

Following the 1963 purchase of the CoG by the Southern, the black-and-imitation-aluminum (Tuxedo) scheme of the parent road was applied to all locomotives. Like other Southern subsidiaries, the CoG was allowed to retain its "Central of Georgia" roadname on the units. Beginning in the late 1960s the "Southern" roadname began to replace the "Central of Georgia," which was relegated to a small "C.G." or "C of G" under the unit number on the cab — a practice that was retained when CoG units were repainted in the Norfolk Southern's Thoroughbred scheme.

Central of Georgia's SD7/9s

Among the Central of Georgia's diesel fleet were one SD7, #201, and six SD9s, nos. 202-207, that had been purchased in 1953 and 1955, respectively — these were to become the only SD7/9s on the Southern roster. With the exception of 1,500-hp for

the SD7 (later rebuilt to 1,750-hp SD9 rating) and 1,750 hp for the SD9s, and a few minor external differences, these units were essentially identical. All weighed in at 368,400 pounds, were 60′ 8½″ long over the couplers, carried 2,400 gallons of fuel oil, 200 gallons of lube oil, 260 gallons of cooling water, and 50 cu. ft. of sand, had a 62:15 gear ratio with a maximum speed of 65 mph on 40″ wheels. Like most diesels owned by the CoG, none had dynamic brakes. External differences included marker lights mounted on a hinged access door on the SD7 as opposed to direct mounting on the SD9, different types of lift rings on the radiator fan housing and cast handrail stanchions on the SD7 compared to stamped ones on the SD9s. There were also four ladders on the SD7 and only three on the SD9 (two on the long hood and one on the short hood). Another almost imperceptible difference was that the steps were more ladder-like on the SD7 and stair-like on the SD9s.

All of the SDs were delivered in the CoG blue-and-gray paint scheme — 201 and 207 were repainted in the Pullman Green scheme in 1960 and units 203 and 205 received similar treatments in 1961. Units 202, 204 and 206 appear to have reached Southern ownership still in the blue-and-gray scheme. Like the rest of the fleet, the SDs were repainted in the Southern tuxedo scheme after 1963 and eventually wore the "Southern" roadname. Units 203-204 and 205-206 were retired and sold in 1978 and 1980, respectively, to the Algiers, Winslow and Western, an Indiana coal hauler half owned by the Southern. Subsequently, 201 was renumbered to 197 and units 202 and 207 were given numbers 198 and 199. Although still on the roster at the time of the merger in 1982, they have since been retired.

The Model

Rail Power Products' (RPP) release of an accurate-width SD7/9 shell without dynamic

brakes gave me the urge to recreate one of these seldom-modeled CoG units in HO scale. Besides, until the RPP shell became available a lot of cutting was required to remove the Athearn dynamic-brake casting — assuming you were able to accept the extra width of the hood. The details on the RPP shell are crisp, well proportioned and relatively free of mold lines. Also, they come with few details — rivets, access doors and air-intake grilles are about all there is! This is both good news and bad news — good because you can add just about any detail you want to match your prototype without having to remove anything first, and bad because of the long list of detail parts you'll need for any prototype. Depending on what parts and chassis you use, I estimate the total cost to range between $90 and $130. Use of the higher-cost parts will, however, result in a model that looks just as good as a brass SD, at half the cost. One compromise you'll have to make if you decide to model the SD7 is the handrails — the Smokey Valley kit comes with the stamped stanchions of the SD9s, but they do have the special "T" junction needed for the stairwell handrails. Had I known this in advance I probably would have modeled one of the SD9s. You might also be able to use the stanchions from a set of GP7 handrails.

Getting Started

Let's begin with a couple of small modifications to the shell before adding any details. I found the hand brake to be the only part on the shell that actually needed replacing. Cut through the back of the hand-brake recess with a sharp knife blade and remove it. Fabricate a new back wall for the recess using sheet styrene and glue in the DW132 hand-brake casting. Although the existing exhaust stacks on the non-dynamic brake insert aren't bad, I decided to replace them with DA2401 stacks. Carve off the existing ones, being careful not to damage the rivets

3 — SD9 #203 shows off the "as-delivered" Central of Georgia paint scheme that was used on diesels from 1946 to 1960. If you look closely you can see the Nathan M3 horn with all chimes facing forward and the single blat horn on the other side of the roof. *Courtesy of Riverdale Station*

4 — Unit 202, an SD9, shows off a wealth of weathering detail. That nice dark blue has faded considerably to a chalky medium blue. *Courtesy of Riverdale Station*

5 — The road grime on unit 207 is even heavier. Notice how the very light gray grime makes the details on those trucks stand out. *Courtesy of Riverdale Station*

6 — This broadside view of SD9 #206 provides another version of the original blue paint before it had weathered much. *Courtesy of Bill Folsom*

7 — Unit 207 shows off the Central of Georgia paint scheme introduced in 1960. *Courtesy of Bill Folsom*

8 — SD7 #201 from a rear angle, in the Pullman Green paint scheme. *Courtesy of Bill Folsom*

9 — Here's #201 again, only in the Southern-inspired paint scheme introduced after the Southern gained ownership in 1963. *Courtesy of Bill Folsom*

10 — By the late 1960s the Southern roadname had been applied to #201 and her sister units, however the Central of Georgia ancestry was evident in the "C. of G." sublettering on the cab. *Courtesy of Bill Folsom*

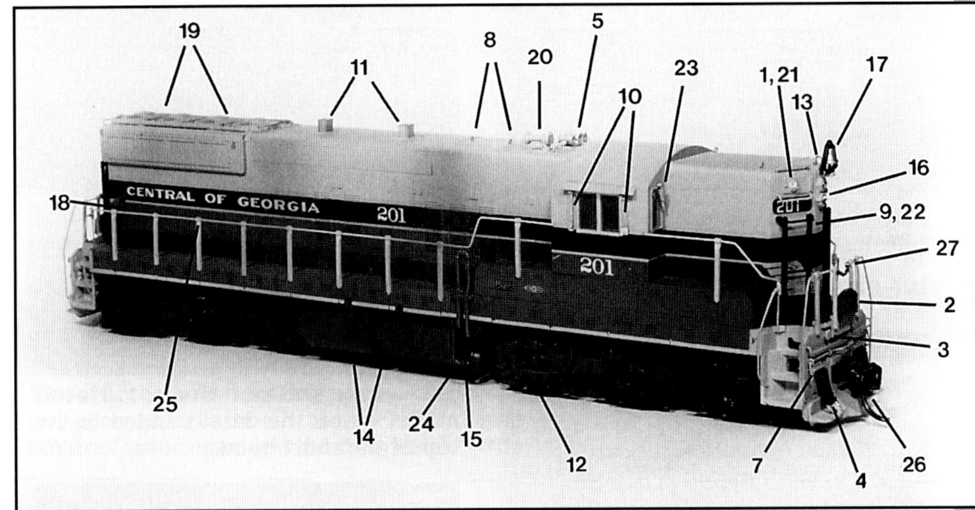

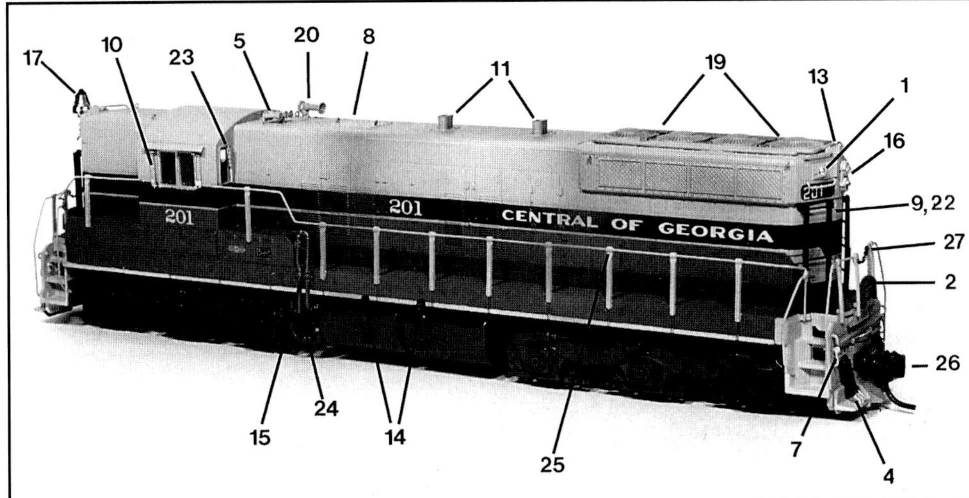

11A & B — The completed unit showing locations of details listed in the Bill of Materials.

Bill of Materials

(Item Numbers refer to Photos 11A and 11B)

Item No.	Part No.	Description
Detail Associates		
1	1018	SD7/9 class lights
2	1402	Drop step
3	1502	MU stand
4	1508	MU hoses*
5	1601	M3 air horn
7	2205	Coupler lift bar
8	2206	Lift rings
9	2207	SD7/9 ladder kit*
10	2312	Cab deflector, prime, straight
11	2401	Exhaust stacks
12	2807	Speed recorder
13	3002	Sand-filler hatch*
14	3102	Fuel-tank fittings
Details West		
15	111	SD7/9 Breather pipe
16	114	Twin sealed-beam casting
17	128	Bell
18	132	Hand brake
19	142	36″ cooling fan
20	173	Blat air horn
13	201	Sand-filler hatch*
MV Products		
21	22	Marker-lamp lens
Overland		
22	9704	SD7/9 ladders
Precision Scale		
23	3968	Windshield wipers
24	48195	Pipe fittings
24	48196	Pipe fittings
Smokey Valley		
25	4	SD9 handrails
Kadee®		
26	5	Couplers
Builders in Scale		
27	250	Black chain
Yellowstone Custom Services		
4	8007	MU hoses*
Microscale Decals		
	87-48	Diesel data
	87-604	Central of Georgia Diesels
Shellscale Decals		
	105	Black numberboards
Accu-flex Paint		
	16-01	Engine Black
	16-03	Grimy Black
	16-12	Primer Gray
	16-19	Soo Line Dulux Gold
	16-20	Super Gloss Black
	16-66	Grand Trunk Western Blue
Clover House		
	244	.0159 brass wire
A-West		
		Blacken It

*Indicates items with multiple choices

at their base, and glue the replacements on. Next glue the hood insert in place. Now grab the cab and drill #76 holes for the eyebolts needed to hold the DA2312 cab wind deflectors and #65 for the PS3968 windshield wipers — install the wipers after painting. I made the cab sunshades from a piece of brass strip left over from a package of brass track connectors. Use a piece with a couple of the small tabs — cut the strip to the right length, bend the tabs to about a 45° angle and glue in place over the cab window. Finally, glue the cab into its slot in the shell.

Let's finish the roof by drilling #76 holes for the lift rings. Don't forget those on the side of the air-intake grille openings — they should go just fore and aft of the grille rivet strip at its top. Glue DA2206 lift rings in all these holes. Once these are in place add the DW142 36″ fans — remember to keep them close to each other or there won't be room for the cooling coil. The cooling coil was fabricated by bending a length of .32-diameter brass rod to the correct shape using the Athearn shell as a template. Drill a couple of .32 holes in the roof and insert the ends of the coil into it. Apply glue sparingly to the underside of the coil and ease it into place. Now add the sand-filler hatches (either DA3002 or DW201) at each end of the

hood. The horns are the final touch to the roof. The CoG used an odd mix of one rear-facing blat-type horn (DW173) along with a Nathan M3 (DA1601) with all chimes facing forward. These were located on the rear of the access plate just behind the cab.

With the exception of the bell on the short hood, the two ends of the locomotive were essentially identical. Attach the DA1018 class lights as shown on the model — it's important to get these positioned correctly since everything else goes on relative to them. The DW114 twin sealed-beam headlight casting is located midway between the two class lights, with about half its length below the bottom of the access door. Drill #76 mounting holes for hand grabs, 24″ apart above and below the class-light access doors. The 24″ hand grabs have to be bent from .0159 diameter brass wire — note that the upper grab is straight whereas the lower one has an angle-like standard drop grab. These should be centered on the angled section of the hood end, making them slightly off center of the access doors.

Drilling the holes for the ladders in the right places can be real guesswork unless you're willing to make a template. This can be as simple as punching holes through a piece of index card or sheet styrene, or go all

Electro-Motive Division (EMD)
Colorado and Southern (C&S) SD9

HO Scale Models by Athearn and
Rail Power Products (shell & chassis only)
N Scale Model by Atlas

by Rich Picariello

Photos from the Houser Collection

The Prototype SD9: The EMD 1,750-hp SD9 was first built in 1954 as a replacement for the 1,500-hp SD7. When production of the SD9 ended in 1959, 471 had been constructed. Both the SD7 and the SD9 ride on EMD's Flexicoil six-wheel trucks. The Colorado and Southern was a fully-owned subsidiary of the Chicago, Burlington and Quincy (CB&Q) and shared a common paint scheme with its parent railroad. C&S SD9s were numbered from 820 to 842 and were delivered between 1956 to 1959. SD9 #828 was equipped with a snowplow and was assigned to the 11,000′-plus altitude of the C&S Leadville-Climax branch. Many C&S SD9s were equipped with steam generators for passenger service when delivered; these were removed in later years.

The Scale Model SD9: The Athearn HO scale SD9 has been available for many years and shows its age with hoods that are wider than scale to accommodate their original wide motor. The body detail still holds up well and Athearn has updated the original metal truck sideframes to more highly-detailed plastic versions. Proto Power West offers a chassis designed for the Athearn shell (#38302, $73). Rail Power Products (RPP) makes a plastic SD7/9 shell, available with or without dynamic brakes, and a cast chassis. Included with the shell as separate parts are either a dynamic or non-dynamic brake hatch, four walkway step guards and four or six fans. The chassis includes these separate parts: an air tank and a half fuel tank. RPP has left off the specific details for either an SD7 or SD9 making the shell usable for either locomotive. All C&S SD9s were equipped with dynamic brakes so use the RPP shell set that has dynamic brakes. RPP's SD7/9 cast chassis is designed to accept Athearn SD9 trucks, motor (or a can motor) and drive-gear components. The chassis has the rear fuel tank molded on with a separate plastic front tank so that locomotives equipped with one fuel tank (Nos. 820 and 821) can be modeled without the need to cut off the forward tank as must be done on the Athearn chassis.

A limited-production SD9 for N scale has been available in the past from Atlas.

Paint and Decal Notes: C&S locomotives were painted in the same colors as their parent, the CB&Q. The early scheme was gray on the upper third of the carbody and black on the lower two-thirds of the carbody, underframe, trucks, fuel tank and lower pilots. Handrails were black with white at the step areas. C&S SD9 #828, following rebuilding after a wreck, was repainted in March 1959 as the first Burlington Route locomotive to wear the new gray-and-Chinese-Red paint scheme. The underframe, handrails and trucks were painted black. The red paints listed in the paint section are needed for the red scheme only.

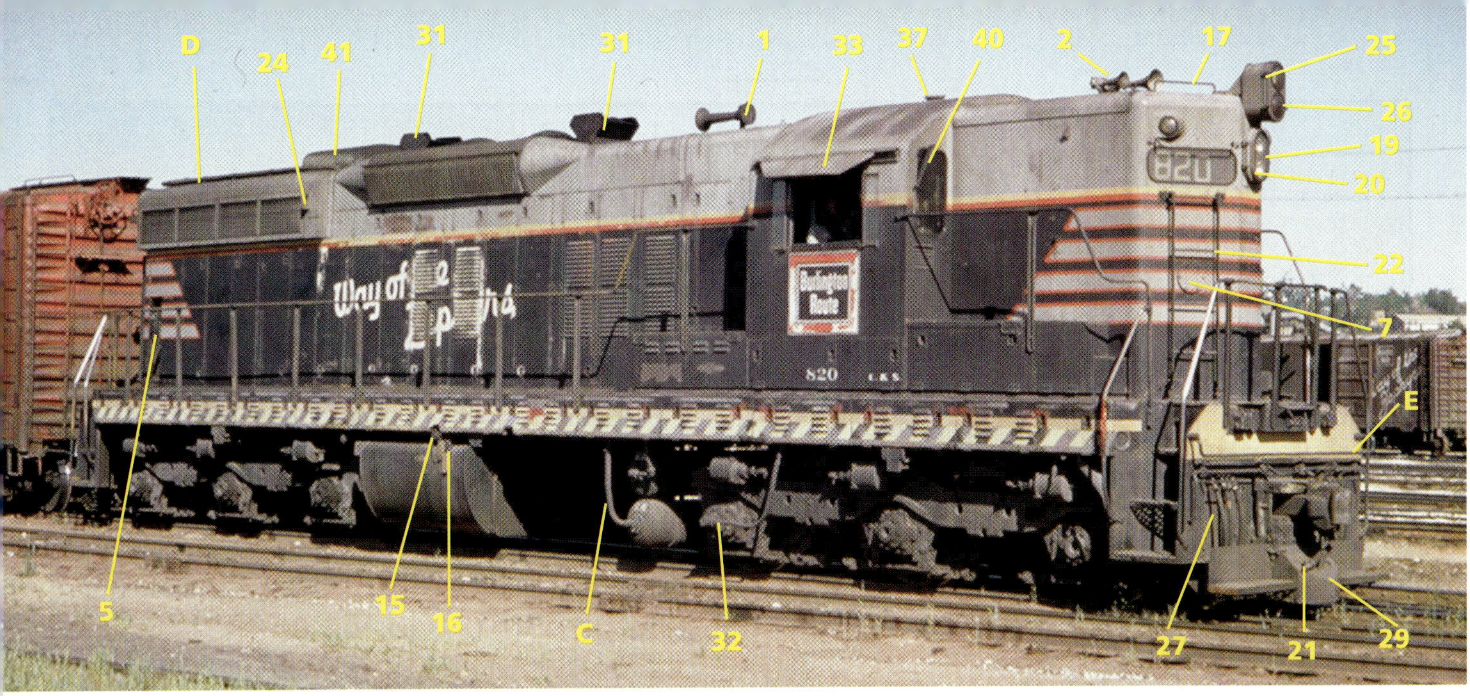

D
24
41
31
31
1
33
37
40
2
17
25
26
19
20
22
7
E
820
Burlington Route
5
15
16
C
32
27
21
29

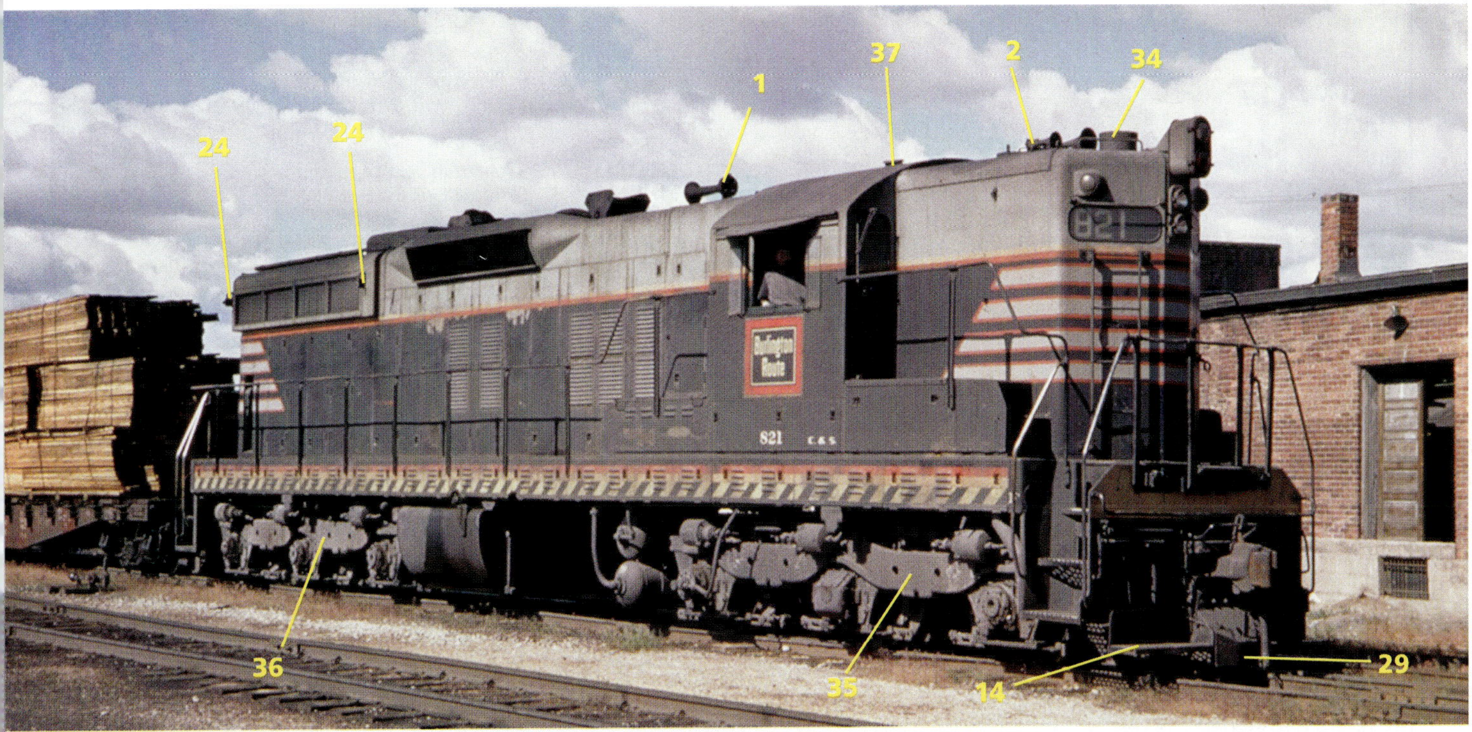

24
24
1
37
2
34
821
Burlington Route
36
35
14
29

30
34
37
39
23
23
12
13
41
13
30
25
824
Burlington Route
A
32
35
15
16
15
36

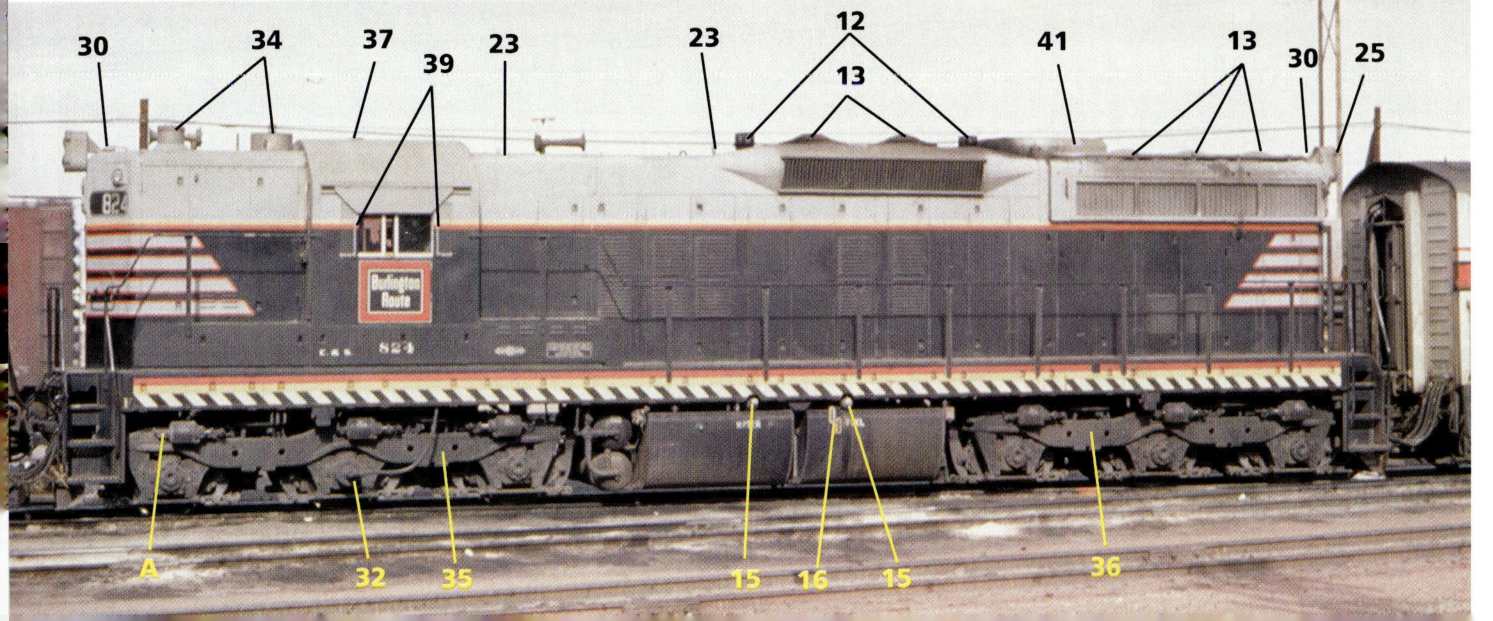

Delaware & Hudson RS11 and RS36

Detail Parts for HO Scale:

1 - CS420   Air horn (brass) . . . . 4.95/ea.
   DA1601   Air horn (delrin) 1.75/2
   DW175   Air horn (brass) . . . . 2.50/ea.
2 - CS422   Air horn, single (brass) 2.50/2
   DW174   Air horn, single (brass) 2.00/2
   Note: On No. 5002 only.
3 - DA3201   Air tanks (plastic)* 2.25/2
   DW204   Air tanks (metal)* 1.95/2
   Note: The tanks may have to be cut shorter.
4 - CF201   Antenna, Sinclair (brass) 3.79/4
   DA1803   Antenna, Sinclair (plastic) 1.25/4
5 - DA1202   Bell, underframe (plastic) 1.00/2
   DW127   Bell, underframe (metal) 1.25/2
6 - DW179   Brake wheel* 1.00/2
7 - DA2210   Chain, blackened . . . . 2.25/12"
   PSC48348   Chain . . . . 2.75/10"
8 - MV20   Classification light lenses* 1.50/4
9 - DA2211   Coupler lift bar 2.00/2
   OM9151   Coupler lift bar 1.95/2
10 - OM9171   Door handle 1.67/2
11 - DA1408   Drop step 3.00/2
12 - CS461   Dynamic brake* . . . . 1.95/ea.
13 - TP1203   Exhaust stack 1.40/2
   Note: This part may not match the large stack on
       D&H units as it is not illustrated in the
       Walthers catalog; it may have to be scratchbuilt.
14 - DA2208   Footboard, pilot* 3.25/2
15 - DA3102   Fuel Filler (plastic)† 1.00/set
   DW166   Fuel filler (metal) 1.00/4
   PSC39080   Fuel filler (plastic) 1.50/4
16 - DA2202   Grabirons 2.50/48
17 - SV45   Handrail set* . . . . 16.95/ea.
18 - DA1024   Headlight* 1.00/2
19 - MV22   Headlight lenses* 1.10/4
20 - CS227   Hose, air line (brass) 2.15/4
   DA6206   Hose, air line (delrin) 1.25/6
21 - DA1107   Lift rings, ALCo 1.25/12
22 - CF257   MU hoses, 3-per bracket (brass) 4.95/4
   DA1508   MU hoses, individual (delrin) 2.00/16
   OM9350   MU hoses, 3-per bracket (brass) 6.10/4
23 - DA1501   MU stand 1.25/2
24 - DW202   Sand-fill hatch (metal)* 1.25/4
   OM9400   Sand-fill hatch (brass)* 3.30/2

25 - CF196   Speed recorder (brass) 4.39/4
   DA2807   Speed recorder (delrin) 1.50/4
26 - CF112   Underframe/step light (brass) 2.95/2
   DW172   Underframe/step light 1.25/8
27 - DA2312   Wind deflector (clear plastic) 1.25/4
   OM9327   Wind deflector (brass) 2.50/4
   UP77   Wind deflector/mirror (brass) 2.00/2
28 - AL29200   Windshield wipers (delrin) 1.75/8
   CS419   Windshield wipers (brass) 3.50/4
   PSC3968   Windshield wipers (plastic) 1.50/4
   UP94   Windshield wipers (brass) 2.00/4
   UP97   Windshield wipers (plastic) 1.50/4

Detail Parts for N Scale:

1 - DA8204   Air horn 1.25/2
   JNJ113   Air horn 3.50/2
   SE-N700   Air horn 1.65/ca
2 - SE-N702   Air horn, single 1.65/2
4 - ME-NA1   Antenna, Sinclair (brass) . . . . 1.70/ea.
   SE-N450   Antenna, Sinclair (brass) 1.65/3
5 - ME-N88   Bell, underframe (brass) . . . . 1.65/ea.
   SE-N351   Bell, underframe (metal) 1.65/2
6 - SE-N698   Brake wheel* 1.70/2
11 - DA8206   Drop step 1.00/2
18 - DA8217   Headlight* 1.25/4
20 - PSC6704   Hose, air line (brass) 1.50/6
   PSC6705   Hose, air line (plastic) 2.50/24
22 - SE-N550   MU hoses 3.95/4
23 - ME-NS4   MU stand . . . . 2.00/?
24 - ME-NH14   Sand-fill hatch . . . . 3.35/?
25 - SE-N499   Speed recorder 1.65/2

The following parts must be fabricated by the modeler:
A — Brake-cylinder air line — simulate with brass wire.
B — File off the intercooler radiators if building an RS32.
C — Various handgrabs — form from brass wire.
D — Overflow hose — make from brass wire.
E — Handbrake chain guides — make from styrene.

† DA3102 Fuel Tank Fittings (set) contains other parts that may or may not be needed for this detailing project.
* Similar parts, either separate or molded on, are included with the Atlas or Model Power scale models; replacement of any or all original parts is left to the discretion of the modeler.

Decals:

HO Scale:

Accucals	5814	(all schemes)
Herald King	L-340	(blue-and-gray scheme)
	L-342	(all-blue scheme w/yellow lettering)
Microscale	87-31	(1970 blue-and-gray scheme)
	87-582	(all-blue '70s to '80s scheme w/yellow lettering)
	87-587	(blue-and-gray '70s to early '90s scheme)
Walthers	934-46760	(blue-and-gray scheme)
	934-46750	(all-blue scheme w/yellow lettering)

N Scale:

Microscale	60-31	(1970 blue-and-gray scheme)
	60-582	(all-blue '70s to '80s scheme w/yellow lettering)
	60-587	(blue-and-gray '70s to early '90s scheme)

Paints:

Accu-flex:	16-01	Engine Black
	16-02	Reefer White
	16-12	Primer Gray (lighten w/white)
	16-76	Delaware & Hudson Blue
Accu+paint:	2	Stencil Black
	5	Delaware & Hudson Blue
	23	Delaware & Hudson Yellow
	47	Delaware & Hudson Gray
Floquil:	110010	Engine Black
	110150	D&H Gray (discontinued)
	110151	D&H Blue (discontinued)
Scalecoat:	8	D&H Yellow
	9	D&H Blue
	10	Black
	63	D&H Gray

AL/ PPW: A-Line/Proto Power West
P.O. Box 7916
La Verne, CA 91750

CS: Cal-Scale
21 Howard Street
Montoursville, PA 17754

CF: Custom Finishing
379 Tully Road
Orange, MA 01364

DA: Detail Associates
Box 5357
San Luis Obispo, CA 93403

DW: Details West
P.O. Box 5132
Hacienda Heights, CA 91745

JNJ: JnJ Trains
P.O. Box 1535
Ottumwa, IA 52501

ME: Miniatures by Eric
RR # 1
Busby, Alberta
Canada TOG OHO

MV: MV Products
P.O. Box 6622
Orange, CA 92667

OM: Overland Models Inc.
3808 W. Kilgore Avenue
Muncie, IN 47304-4896

PSC: Precision Scale Company
3961 Hwy. 93 North
Stevensville, MT 59870

SE: Sunrise Enterprises
P.O. Box 172
Doyle, CA 96109

SV: Smokey Valley Railroad Products
P.O. Box 339
Plantersville, MS 38862

TP: Trackside Parts
55 Alvin Street
Providence, RI 02907

UP: Utah Pacific
9520 E. Napier Avenue
Benton Harbor, MI 49022

Note: These detail parts may be available at your local hobby dealer(s), so try there first. If you must order directly from a manufacturer, include at least $3.50 for postage and handling. You must purchase the full quantities as shown in the detail parts list.

Gulf Summit Pushers
MODELING
ERIE-LACKAWANNA F3s

by Jim Six

Photos by the author

The Erie-Lackawanna typically utilized a pair of EMD covered wagons as pushers up to Gulf Summit. One could imagine that the 7101 and 7141 have just completed a push upgrade and are drifting back downhill to assist yet another train over the hill. The clouds and trees add significantly to the realism of this photo of the models. Both models are manufacturer-painted Stewart Hobbies F3s that have been enhanced with commercially available detail parts, a few paint changes and some weathering.

Hearing the horn of an approaching train Jer and I ran toward the tracks to gain a better vantage point. A few minutes earlier Dad had pulled our new Pontiac Catalina into a Sinclair station for gas and pop. It was October 1962, and we were headed for Mohigan State Forest for a day of hiking and picnicking — burgers and some end-of-summer sweet corn. The trees were starting to turn, and I was relieved that we weren't going to church that morning. I hated getting dressed up, especially having to wear a white shirt and tie.

Breathing heavily, we positioned ourselves at the edge of the ditch that paralleled the tracks just as the train's headlight probed from around the bend through the morning mist. *Blat. Blaaaat.... Blat.* The engineer reached out the open cab window and motioned with an animated salute toward us as he passed. But it wasn't the engineer that had my attention. It was the lead diesel he commanded. I was taken aback that the engine wasn't black and yellow. Huh? Aren't Erie diesels supposed to be black with yellow? Through partly obscured by the morning haze, it was apparent that the lead engine was yellow, maroon and gray. Then it passed amidst a roar and cloud of dust. She must have been laying down sand for traction. It stuck in my mind that the name on the sides of that diesel was LACK-AWANNA. No familiar Erie diamond. But there was little time to stand around in wonder as Dad was beckoning us.

That was more than 30 years ago, and a lot has changed in railroading since then. Now F3s are diesels we buy from Lionel or Stewart, and the only railroad in Ashland is an industrial shortline that operates the pared down remainder of what was inherited from Conrail. The Erie became the Erie-Lackawanna which became part of Conrail in 1976. Shortly thereafter the western end of the old Erie was dismembered and either abandoned piece by piece or transferred over to a few enterprising organizations that tried to continue rail service on a limited basis.

Although I didn't know it at the time, that boyhood railroad encounter was my introduction to the Erie-Lackawanna Railroad. In those early 1960s encounters most all of the locomotives in Ashland remained in black-and-yellow paint and either didn't receive EL diamonds or I just didn't notice — probably some of both. It wasn't until the early 1970s that I learned that the Erie and the Lackawanna railroads had merged. Actually, it wasn't until about that time that I became seriously interested in the prototype!

The 1960 merger of the Erie and the Delaware, Lackawanna and Western railroads was the first big eastern merger of the post World War II era — it certainly was not the last! Its initial success, albeit limited, induced others to follow. It wasn't long before the N&W took over the Nickel Plate and the Wabash; the New York Central and Pennsylvania railroads disappeared beneath coats of black and green paint; and a few years later the B&O and C&O joined to form the Chessie System and all of my boyhood favorites were gone.

That's one of the things that makes model railroading so appealing. We can turn back the calendar and put steamers, F-units and other long-retired equipment back into service. The degree of our success is only limited by our abilities and resources. In this case I believe that as far as the locomotives go, I have done rather well. What do you think?

After more than three decades my interest in the Erie-Lackawanna was rekindled by several books about the Erie-Lackawanna, first by Preston Cook's book on the EL focused about Marion (Ohio), then by the three-book series on the E-L by Larry DeYoung. Had these books not been all-color affairs, I might not have been so swayed, but seeing bright yellow, gray and maroon diesels was too much to ignore. Propelled by the enthusiasm generated by those books I set out to obtain every book on the E-L that I could uncover — hard and soft cover, black-and-white and color. I also began to squirrel away some HO scale diesels that were to be become part of my time machine to reconstruct the Erie-Lackawanna. I even completed an Atlas/Kato C425 detailed and painted to represent an Erie-Lackawanna locomotive.

Then came the big dilemma. With my interests so divided among several railroads in two different settings — north vs. southeast — I was in a quandary as to where to direct my increasingly precious resources. Huh? What brought this on? During work on my Erie-Lackawanna C425 and as yet unfinished C424 I noticed that I was having some difficulty seeing what I was doing. No, there was plenty of light. But detail parts, small drills, and other necessary ingredients for preparing prototype models were becoming increasingly difficult to focus on. My goodness...I'm over 40! I am getting old! I thought this would never happen to me. I never really considered that I would become physically impaired. Time for bifocals and an Optivisor®.

There is also the obstacle caused by the escalating cost of models. The days of a good $15 diesel are history. It wasn't too many years ago that I could prepare a Kato-manufactured diesel with all of the goodies for fifty bucks. Now the price tag has

The Erie black-and-yellow paint is a classic, even after modification to represent a transitional Erie-Lackawanna scheme. Note that it doesn't say ERIE in those diamonds, but instead there is the combined E and L! The fact that the fuel tank skirts have been removed is apparent. When you do this, the fuel tank section has to be cut down to match the prototype appearance. This is nearly impossible to do on an Athearn F7 with its integral fuel tank/frame that is cast in hard metal, but this feature is easily duplicated on a Stewart F-unit.

Shown here is the engineer's side of Erie-Lackawanna phase-4 F3 number 7101. Other than the locomotive number, the only way to distinguish this locomotive from an F7 is that there is no cooling fan atop the dynamic brake roof panel, but instead the twin vent screens (barely shown). Stewart's painters did a nice job on the stainless-steel grilles. Also shown is the backup light and other detail of the trailing locomotive.

It's 1965 and Erie-Lackawanna 7141, a former New York, Ontario and Western locomotive, heads a time freight along the famous Southern Tier route across upstate New York. Weathered models need not mean flat finish and cruddy appearance. Jim has been trying different methods for years before finally succeeding in achieving the desired effect. Have you noticed the grabs up the front of the nose? The cast-in relief behind the chicken wire clearly shows the carbody openings. Considering this is all from a mold without separate chicken wire, we are very impressed. How about you?

exceeded a hundred dollars, and prices are still going up. I am having to be more judicious with how I utilize both physical and monetary resources. I can't have everything. As a direct result of my concern over deteriorating eyesight and escalating costs I am preparing diesels at a faster pace than ever before. I'm getting them while I still can. Another result of this is that I am narrowing my modeling focus to southeastern subjects — ACL, CRR, L&N, N&W, SAL and SCL, primarily Atlantic Coast Line and Seaboard

Air Line with the others as supporting cast. It is not that I'll never again model northern subjects — when my southeastern needs are satisfied and if I can still see well enough to build models and if I can still afford then, then there may be more. Until then there will only be these few that I have already started and are near completion, such as the two Erie-Lackawanna F3s featured here.

To acquire enough models to build a southeastern roster I have traded away 14 of my 15 Conrail diesels, keeping only the little

GP15-1. I also swapped away all of my New York Central and Pennsy power. All that remains of my now decimated northern roster are three B&O Fs, two PC Fs, a NKP switcher and a B&LE SD18 — all of which will be used in operating sessions on friends' layouts. Sad as it is to me, the rest are history.

The next step in my great metamorphosis was to set into motion a program of building southeastern locomotives. Starting with but three lonely diesels from Dixie, in fewer

This going-away view of 7141 again clearly shows the effectiveness of the cast-in chicken-wire detail. It is also evident that the high, shrouded fans have been replaced with low, pan-top fans. The crowded rear ends of the locomotives add to the close-coupling effect of the models.

As time passed further into the 1960s esthetics gave way to practicality. As with most other railroads, the Erie-Lackawanna began to pay little attention to the orientation of trailing locomotives, and finding F-units operating elephant style became a common sight. Most modelers won't couple their locomotives this way because they don't like the way it looks. I agree, but if you are to create realistic operating sessions such less-than-appealing configurations are a must. Note that the roof, pilot and trucks are weathered with various shades of grime, but the flanks and nose of the locomotive shine!

than 12 months I now have the count up to 19 and growing. As I said, I'm cranking them out faster than ever.

My two Erie-Lackawanna F3s were loose ends that were near completion when I decided to commit to the southeast. The Erie-Lackawanna being one of my favored among favorite northern subjects and with buddy Mark Olsten in need of early E-L power, I decided to finish them and probably keep them. At this time I have no plans to sell or trade them away, but you know how things go; if someone makes a high enough offer, they too may leave the stable. Most anything can be sold if the price is right!

Mark has a really nice basement-sized railroad with Binghampton, New York, as the focal point. Both Conrail and Erie-Lackawanna operating sessions are planned. Since most of his time has been devoted to layout building he has precious few locomotives — not enough for the operating sessions he dreams of! That's where Earl Murphy, other friends and I along with our EL, PC, and Conrail locomotives fit in.

My two Erie-Lackawanna F3s were prepared for operating sessions set anytime in the 1960s. After an initial surge to paint its diesels, the E-L became financially

The American Limited diaphragm assemblies really show their stuff here — as do the several other details. That the models are "close-coupled" greatly increases the realism of the models. It is regrettable that there is no practical way to connect the MU-hoses on a layout model!

strapped and all but stopped repainting its locomotives. Many units lasted right up into Conrail in their original Erie or transitional black-and-yellow paint.

One of the locomotives that I chose to model has an interesting history. Gray-maroon-and-yellow 7141 represents a phase-2 F3 that was acquired by the Erie from the bankrupt Ontario and Western following its late 1957(?) breakup. It was from a group of phase-2 chicken-wire F3s that were the most modern power on the O&W. The Erie repainted her into its standard Erie black-and-

yellow paint, and other than unit number, the only way to recognize it among original Erie look-alikes was that the former O&W locomotives had the larger (F7-type) bug-eye number boards. Sometime in the 1960s E-L repainted it into former Lackawanna colors with ERIE LACKAWANNA spelled out on its flanks. By then the hyphen had been dropped from the railroad name.

F3 7101 has a less "colorful" history — pun intended! From ground level it appears to be just another F7. But its unit number tells us otherwise. Also, a look-down view would reveal the telltale dynamic brake vents on the roof in place of the 36″ cooling fan found on early F7s. Actually, at first glance the model appears to be just another Erie F-unit. However, a closer look reveals that its diamonds have been changed. Its original diamonds had ERIE spelled out in the center. My model displays the locomotive as it appeared shortly after the 1960 merger with two different transitional diamonds. The nose herald is black with a white center and the combined E and L is in black. The side heralds are yellow diamonds with a black center and yellow combined E and L. This arrangement was concocted to fit in with the Erie paint scheme. Many an

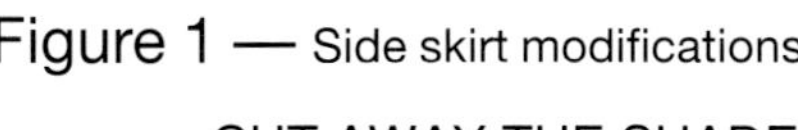

Figure 1 — Side skirt modifications

observer back in the early 1960s and now with my model have mistaken locomotives in this transitional scheme to be just another Erie locomotive — and understandably so!

Of all of the HO scale diesels available I find the Stewart F-units to be my favorite. I roster 17 of them — far more than any other model — and the number is growing. So, it must be so. Until the FT (which as yet I have not seen) all Stewart Fs are manufactured and powered by Kato. This means that their overall appearance and performance are the hobby standard for others to follow. Factory paint in most every case is good to excellent, only Life-Like's PROTO 2000 models may have nicer paint on a consistent basis (my opinion). To prove my point that Stewart's factory-applied paint is so good, both of my EL Fs are factory painted. Really! Sure, I did some tweaking, but that's a whole lot easier than starting from bare gray plastic. Look at the accompanying photos and answer honestly...what do you really think?!

Steve Stewart's line of Electro-Motive F-units is the most comprehensive coverage of any type of diesel locomotive by any manufacturer...and as already stated, done to a very high standard. Prototype F-units matching Stewart's models include the FT A and B (not yet released), F2 A and B, F3 phase-1 A and B, F3 phase-2 A and B, F3 phase-3 A and B, F3 phase-4 A and B, F5 A and B, early F7 A and B, late F7 A and F9 A. The only somewhat serious missing link is an intermediate F7 with the late Farr-type stainless-steel grilles but with horizontal-type louvers between the side portholes. At that, I don't know if any road other than the Atlantic Coast line had any of these intermediate F7s. Not only that, the A-units are available with single or dual headlights. I only wish that the models were also available with or without dynamic brakes! Not even the Atlas/Kato ALCos are as comprehensive as Stewart's EMD Fs. Wouldn't it be nice if we also had EMD E-units with this kind of coverage? Then there are the various versions of GP7 and GP9 units. Such thoughts make my heart throb!

To me, the Stewart Hobbies F-unit is the most significant model locomotive available. Such a strong impact have the Stewart F-units had on me that along with switching to the southeast, I have all but abandoned contemporary modeling and reverted back to the years of my youth, back when Elvis was nothing but a hound dog, back before the British invasion of John, Paul, George, Ringo and others...back before Vietnam was ever heard of. The only heavy metal we knew of was that of our proud American industries.

Something I never really thought about is that the amount of time needed to prepare a good F-unit is about a third to half that of a hood unit, i.e., Geeps and SDs. An evening or two and you have one darned nice model locomotive. The (project) end is in sight right from the very beginning, so you don't have to worry about becoming bogged down and abandoning the project. I know. I've been there many times!

Each model here received the same basic treatment — Details West white metal dress-up kits along with a full compliment of grabirons and various other commercially

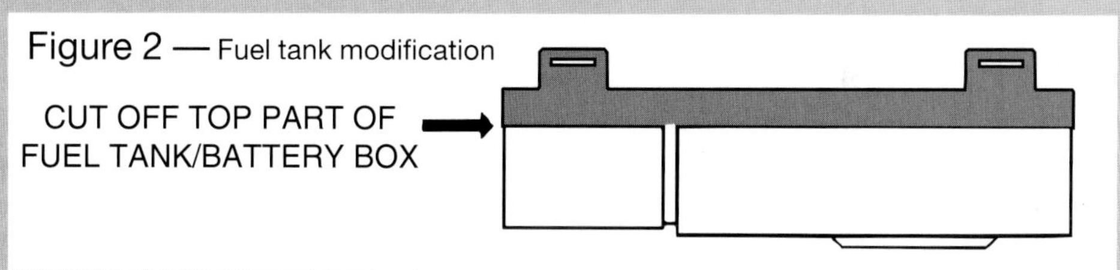

Figure 2 — Fuel tank modification

available detail parts needed to match each model's specific prototype. Each started out as a factory painted model, so some tweaking was called for. The 7101 got new diamonds (as already described), unit numbers on the bug-eye number boards and on the rear flanks of the sides, and stainless steel (decals) between the railings leading up to the cab doors.

My model of Erie-Lackawanna 7141 came as a phase-2 F3 with high shrouded cooling fans. I believe that this is the same configuration used on the prototype 7141 until sometime in the early 1960s when the fans were changed to later pan-top fans (that Stewart includes on its later version F-units). To come up with the configuration that included low fans I replaced the snap-out high-fan unit with Stewart's low-fan replacement (they are interchangeable and available directly from Stewart Hobbies). You could also carve off the shrouded fans and replace them with Details West pan-top replacement fans. Or...you could simply leave the high shrouded fans in place!

We are not done with the 7141 just yet. I felt that the maroon color applied by the manufacturer was too dark and too brown. This was addressed by masking around the maroon area and spray painting over it with Accu+paint EL Maroon. Accu+cals Erie-Lackawanna covered wagon decals were applied for the RADIO EQUIPPED graphic and the long narrow yellow pinstripe running nearly the length of the maroon area. Some work, but much better than having to

start with an undecorated model.

Of the two models the ERIE unit came with the best paint although I felt that the name ERIE in the diamonds was a might hefty — kind of like boldface print. If you are preparing a virgin Erie model I recommend the diamonds be replaced with those found on Microscale's latest Erie diesel decal set. In the case of my model, they were replaced with Accu+cals Erie-Lackawanna diamonds. Other than the diamond swap and some weathering, the yellow-and-black model displays its manufacturer-applied paint.

With paint adjusted to suit my fancy, a more or less standard assortment of detail was added which included formed-wire grabs and railings, radio antennas, lift rings, sand hoses, speed recorder and coupler cut levers both front and back. I also added back-end detail including diaphragms from American Limited — a first for me. I wasn't disappointed either. As was done on the prototype, I removed the fuel tank/battery box skirting from the sidesills exposing the fuel tank. This meant that the fuel tank had to be modified to appear like the prototype.

To remove the skirting from the sides of the locomotive models I used Rail Nippers®, then trimmed the rough cuts with a sharp X-Acto® knife. Figure 1 shows the areas to be cut away (shaded). Studying both Erie and Lackawanna photos it appears that most side skirts were modified during the very late 1950s, though some lasted into the 1960s.

Once the skirts have been removed the fuel tank assembly is exposed. You will immediately notice the very unprototypical appearance of the snap-on mounts for holding the fuel tank to the cast metal drive unit frame. Remove the fuel tank and cut away the unwanted upper area (shown in Figure 2). Use Hobsco Goo® to hold the modified fuel tank to the drive unit.

I made a little special effort in photographing these two models for a few reasons. This will be my last article on northeastern subjects for some time — who knows, maybe ever. And secondly, I have been experimenting with some new photography techniques and believe that I have them down pat. This article and accompanying photos are solely intended to inspire and motivate readers. Hopefully my efforts will prompt you to take a stab at preparing enhanced models of your own. As you have seen, scratchbuilding and kitbashing are not necessary to come up with realistic models that are wonderfully convincing when placed in the appropriate setting. Happy modeling!   **I**

By Stuart R. Thayer

Photos by the author unless otherwise indicated

The BL2 was the ugliest locomotive ever built! This is the comment I hear from a great many prototype and model railroad enthusiasts. Do I agree with this sentiment? Not really. I will admit that the BL2 is an awkward-looking locomotive, and it has a face that probably only a mother could love. However, at the same time it is a distinctively unique locomotive that peaks my interest. There has never been another diesel locomotive produced that has ever resembled it. The BL2 definitely stands alone.

Aesthetics aside, on a functional level the BL2 was a dismal failure. Essentially, it was an F-unit rearranged for branchline duty. Though the idea was sound, the result was not. The BL2 never really lived up to its designers' ambitions. However, it did succeed in teaching the EMD designers many valuable lessons that eventually manifested themselves in the incredibly successful GP7. The inadequacies of the BL2 have been documented many times before, so I will not belabor the point here.

Having been born and raised in the southern terminus of the Monon Railroad, Louisville, KY, it was only natural that I would become acquainted with, and interested in the "Hoosier Line." In addition, the Kentucky Railway Museum, that was located in Louisville at that time, had Monon BL2 #32 in their collection. This allowed me the opportunity to examine an authentic piece of Monon motive power whenever I wanted. Later on, after I turned 16 and got my driver's license, I began railfanning the southern end of the former Monon Route and became increasingly interested in

Indiana's own railroad. In addition, Mont Switzer and Bill Darnaby constantly reinforced my interest over the years with their wonderful articles on modeling the Monon. So, when Life-Like introduced the BL2 in their Proto 2000 series, and made it available in a Monon paint scheme, I knew it wouldn't be long before I had one. So, let's talk about building a model of one of these distinctive locomotives as they appeared on the Monon in the late 1960s.

The first thing I considered in building this model was that I wanted to save as much of the original paint as possible since Life-Like did an outstanding job. With that in mind, I went to my reference materials and started looking up information on the Monon's BL2s. Luckily, there are two wonderful books available, *Monon Route* by George Hilton and *Monon; The Hoosier Line* by Gary and Stephen Dolzall.

The Monon rostered nine BL2s, numbered 30-38. Numbers 30-35 were built in April 1948 and 36-38 were built in May 1949. The Monon owned the second-largest roster of BL2s behind the C&O, which owned 15. An interesting fact about the Monon's BL2s is that according to the May/June 1974 *Extra 2200 South*, #30 was the first BL2 produced and #38

was the last. They were all painted in the classic black-and-gold Purdue University paint scheme. Aside from the all-time classics such as the Santa Fe Warbonnet, this was one of the more interesting paint schemes to come along in my books.

With information in hand, I put together a list of details that needed to be added or changed to bring the model up to the level of accuracy I was looking for. (A side comment here is that the Life-Like BL2 is a near-perfect representation of a Western Maryland BL2 as they appeared in the late 1960s through 1970s.)

Lets start by removing a few things in preparation for adding new details. Trim the ladder grabs on both sides of the nose flush with the body. Remove the sunshade assemblies and fill the resulting holes with your favorite putty. I prefer automobile spot putty, which is available at any automotive paint store and some automotive parts stores. Also remove the piping arrangement on the top rear of the long hood and a portion of the lower skirting on both sides. Refer to the photos to see how much to remove. Trim off the portion of the hand grab on top of the nose that extends back towards the cab. I did not replace all the existing grabirons and railings. I was not interested in a wholesale reworking of the model; I simply wanted to correct and add to what was already there. The Life-Like railings are a little oversized, but the detail is right, and I was satisfied to leave them as is. Lastly, remove the MU receptacle detail and fill the holes. At this point I will offer a word

Monon BL2 #32 in Hammond, IN.
Photographer unknown, Stuart Thayer collection

Monon BL2 #36 in K&IT Youngtown Yard, Louisville, KY.
Photographer unknown, Stuart Thayer collection

of caution. The trainline castings on each pilot are susceptible to being broken off while handling the model as modifications and detailing progresses. I know, I broke both of them off, and I was being careful. If I had it to do over again, I would figure out some way of removing them all together and remounting them after all major work was done.

Now we are ready to start adding details. Begin by adding all the necessary lift rings on the unit's roof and a set of long grabirons over the side windows. These grabs are approximately .630 long with a center support. I used an eyebolt for the support. These grabs should be centered on the side doors. The last item to finish off the roof is a firecracker antenna offset to the fireman's side toward the rear of the cab.

Some other details to be considered before we move to the pilots and truck sideframes are the cab awnings and headlights. The headlights are a simple matter of drilling and filing out the existing castings to except MV LS11 lenses. The cab awnings are a little more involved. See Figure 1. Start by making two brackets out of .012 brass wire. Next cut two pieces of .005 styrene sheet. These will be the foundations for the canvas awnings. Drill #80 holes approximately .165 from the top of the cab side wall on either side of the window opening, and mount the brackets and foundations as shown. Next cut two pieces of bathroom tissue the same size as the .005 styrene awning foundations. Laminate these on to the foundations. Do this by first carefully spot gluing them with fast penetrating CA. After that has dried, saturate the tissue with more CA until both pieces are sufficiently secured to the styrene. After these are painted the tissue will give the effect of a canvas awning. As shown, they are fully extended. However, I'm

sure some industrous soul out there will think up a way to model them in a fully or partially folded position.

The next areas to consider are the pilots. First remove the existing castings for the coupler cut-lever bar. Continue #79 holes through the depressions that arc left and form coupler cut bars from .012 brass wire. I had to form my own because the Detail Associates part that I normally like to use were not long enough to line up with the holes. Use some of the new DA2222 long eyebolts to mount the cut-lever bars. The long eyebolts will allow you to mount them far enough off the face of the pilot to align correctly with the draft-gear buffer. Next, install five MU hoses on either side of the coupler opening.

One last item concerning the pilots is the couplers. I chose to body mount them. To do this you will need to build a mounting pad out of styrene inside the shell, and cut off the existing frame-mounting pads and the ends of the underframe that will interfere with the new mounting pads. By doing this you can then permanently attach the pilot steps and still be able to remove the shell for maintenance.

The drop steps and new MU receptacles are next. The drop steps are a simple matter. All we need here is to remove the center horizontal framing from the underside of both steps. This allows for the placement of the units road number later. Lastly, you will need to build four new MU receptacle assemblies (see Figure 2). These are mounted on either side of the drop step.

Details added to the trucks include a DA2807 speed recorder on the rear axle of the engineer's side front truck, sand lines and air piping between the cylinders.

With all detailing and modifications done, the unit is ready for some touch-up painting.

Besides painting all the new details, there are some features of the paint job that need to be painted out. These include the "Wheel-on-Rail" herald below the cab windows and the C.I.L. (Chicago, Indianapolis & Louisville) reporting marks next to the rear number boards. The Monon dropped the Chicago, Indianapolis & Louisville as their corporate title on January 11, 1956. From that point on, the railroad was known simply as Monon. As for the herald, Life-Like did a wonderful job, and I hated to paint it out, however I have found only one photo that shows a BL2 with that exact style of herald. Page 19 of the Dolzall book shows #36 heading toward Lafayette with a local in 1960 with this herald. So this logo is appropriate for an early '60s model of #36. However, by the late '60s #36 had lost its distinctive herald. Thus, out came the airbrush, and with a few sprays of Floquil Gold it was gone.

Paint all handrails, stanchions and grabirons yellow. In addition, all sideframe step, pilot step and cab-side ladder step edges are yellow. The cab awnings and all hoses were painted Grimy Black; the glad hands were painted Old Silver as were the cab-side ladder kick plates, the truck sideframes and the site glass and fuel-filler frames. The emergency fuel shut off was painted Signal Red. Oh, I almost forgot, don't forget to paint the crew.

With the painting finished, you will need to add a couple additional decals. These are; EMD builder's plates from Microscale, a small "F" on each side just behind the pilot areas, and road numbers to the underside of the drop steps. I used some leftover numbers from a Model Railroad Supply Monon decal set #1W, Modern Freight Lettering/White.

At this point, we are ready for the finishing touch; weathering. By the late 1960s the Monon's BL2s had seen a lot of hard work, and most of the photos I have seen show them with a considerable amount of road grime and overall grunge. Yet at the same time, they didn't look like rolling junk. Monon maintenance people took pride in their railroad. So, weather accordingly. I used a mixture of artist's pastels and chalks with airbrushed weathering colors.

Upon finishing, you can ask the question, "Was the BL2 really the ugliest locomotive ever built?" Who cares! The Monon's ugly ducklings will always hold a certain fascination and fondness in my heart. ∎

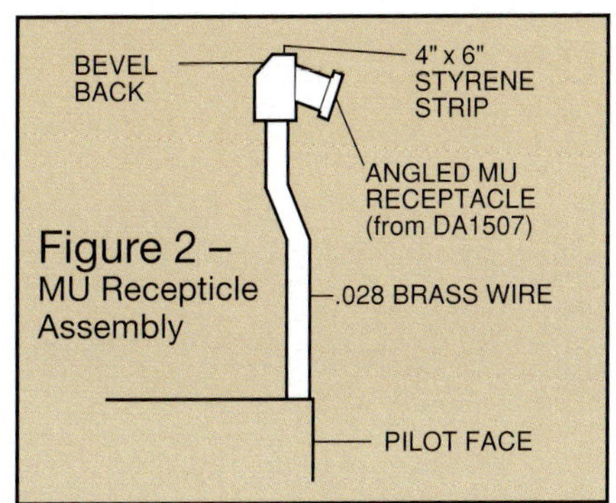

Electro-Motive Division (EMD) New York Central (NYC) GP30

HO Scale Model by Bachmann
N Scale Model by Atlas

by Rich Picariello

Photos from the Houser Collection

The Prototype GP30: EMD introduced the 2,250-hp GP30 in 1961. When production ended in 1963, 908 units had been built. The GP30 represented a radical styling departure from earlier EMD hood units, the most obvious feature being the distinctive streamlined housing covering the dynamic-brake resistors and the air system. Most GP30s rode on EMD Blomberg type B four-wheel trucks. A few railroads' GP30s rode on traded-in ALCo AAR type B trucks. Forty cabless GP30B units were also built for the Union Pacific. Some of the UP B units carried steam generators for passenger service; no other GP30s were so equipped.

Diesel locomotives of NYC's "Water Level Route" did not normally need dynamic brakes and none of their 10 GP30s had them. Acquired by the NYC in 1962, these units were last numbered from 2190 to 2200 before the Penn Central merger.

The Scale Model GP30: The former Lionel HO scale GP30 is now made by Bachmann and is available as a Spectrum limited-availability super-detailed model. Spectrum models have a better motor and drive system than the regular run of Bachmann diesel locomotives and, in addition, feature many free-standing detail parts (as opposed to cast-on details such as grabirons). Older Bachmann (non-Spectrum) GP30s and the Lionel GP30 can often be found for bargain prices at model railroad hobby shops, swap meets, auctions or flea markets. An undecorated Spectrum model would be best, requiring only paint, decals

and the addition of the listed NYC-specific detail parts making this an easy project for those just starting diesel detailing.

Atlas has recently released a new GP30 for N scale that features a smooth-running mechanism and fine details; GP30 models made by Atlas (an earlier model) and Rapido have been available in the past.

Any of the above listed models will require filling in the dynamic-brake grids to represent a non-dynamic-brake NYC GP30.

Paint and Decal Notes: NYC diesels were painted all black with white sidesills. Yellow paint is used on the step-area handrails, all handgrabs and the step edges. Note that 2193 has all-yellow handrails with black stanchions. This was the last scheme used before the merger of the Pennsylvania and New York Central to form the Penn Central.

27
34
35
2
2
21
14
11
15
NEW YORK CENTRAL
2191
2191
2191
CENTRAL
SYSTEM
23
4
20
19
1
34
33
5
6
8
29
10
30

27
27
7
27
17
16
17
27
21
22
30
24
25
34
35
12
28
NEW YORK CENTRAL
2193
2193
2193
CENTRAL
33
19
4
32
A
B
13
18
10
26
18
29

The original stack was retained on the model of SAL 1426. The distinctive square exhaust stack that was added to SAL 1426 sometime in the late '50s and remained until retirement could easily be fabricatd from styrene.

SAL 1426 is seen here in Hamlet, NC, sometime in the early 1960s after it received its "home-made" stack. This unit's paint scheme matches the one found on the Atlas model.

Warren Calloway photo, courtesy of Diesel Era *magazine*

Notice the different paint scheme and stack on SAL 1425. The sidesill is red, the cab roof is black and the red on the hood in front of the cab doesn't go over the top.

Warren Calloway collection, courtesy of Diesel Era *magazine*

The rear of SAL 1426. Hamlet, NC; October 22, 1967.
Warren Calloway photo, courtesy of Diesel Era *magazine*

SCL 42, the former SAL 1426, still retains remnants of its SAL paint in 1968. Hamlet, NC; July 13, 1968.
Warren Calloway photo, courtesy of Diesel Era *magazine*

SCL 42 still sports its square stack, but has been repainted and has lost the conduit that goes to the antenna base. Hamlet, NC; July 3, 1970.
Warren Calloway photo, courtesy of Diesel Era *magazine*

Seaboard Air Line ALCo S2 Locomotive Roster

SAL	SCL	B/D	Remarks
1403	NA	Jan 42	Retired Jul 66
1404	NA	Jan 42	Retired Jul 66
1405	NA	Apr 42	Retired Jul 66
1425	41	Aug 46	Retired Aug 76
1426	42	Aug 46	Retired Dec 76
1427	43	Aug 46	Retired Jul 76
1428	44	Aug 46	Retired Dec 75
1429	45	Sep 46	Retired Aug 76
1430	46	Sep 46	Retired Aug 76
1431	47	Sep 46	Retired Jul 78
1432	48	Jun 48	Retired Aug 76
1433	49	Jun 48	Retired Aug 76
1434	50	Jun 48	Retired Aug 76

The first step in enhancing the Atlas S2 (or S4) should be to carve off all cast-on grabirons and replace them with formed-wire replacements like those offered by Detail Associates, A-Line or Tichy. If you have done this before and are working with an undecorated model, then this should offer no difficulty. However, in my case I was working with a factory-painted model and did not want to damage its paint any more than absolutely necessary. To remove the grabs I used a chisel-type X-Acto® blade, taking care not to gouge the surface. The rough areas where the grabs were removed were then scraped and sanded smooth. Holes were drilled for the replacement grabs which were then pressed into place and secured with CA cement. The part of the grabs that extend through the body to the inside were then cut off or bent over to prevent them from interferring with moving drive parts or the fit of the body onto the drive unit.

I have harped about Atlas's arcane practice of offering quality locomotives with cast-on grabs for quite some time. So you can imagine my pleasure at learning that their new U33/36C will be their first locomotive to be released sans cast-on grabs. Since I doubt they will change the dies for their existing locomotives, modelers who want to eliminate the toy-like appearance of the cast-on grabs will still have to carve them off and replace each with formed-wire replacements on their present models. Believe me, the result is well worth the effort. On the down side is the fact that the red bands across the nose will be ruined in the process and will have to be re-applied — either with paint or (Microscale Seaboard) decals. I also carved off the four engine-compartment hood lift rings and replaced them with formed-wire versions.

Let's give Atlas credit for those one-piece cast railing/stanchion sections. They're pretty darned good. The only parts of the railings that I found objectionable were the ends where they turn down alongside the step wells and the two railings leading up to the back door of the cab. I first replaced the back-door railings with .019 brass rod, then cut away the end sections of the railings. Holes were drilled into the stanchions exactly where the railings were cut off, then

.019 brass rod sections were formed as replacements. Each section was then pressed into the holes (that had just been drilled) at the top of the stanchions. A dab of CA cement held everything in place. I find that replacing the end sections and leaving the main railings alone is a good compromise that sacrifices little, yet gains a lot.

Next I added a radio antenna base and conduit. The antenna base was cemented to the cab roof along the centerline about a scale two feet from the front edge. A .015 brass rod was used to represent the conduit. It was bent 90° so that it ran horizontally from the front of the antenna base forward about a scale four feet before turning straight down into the top of the hood. A single strand of stranded wire was cut and cemented to the antenna base to represent the antenna whip. I suggest leaving this off until the model is ready to be placed on the layout and left alone except for operation on the pike. The whip is easily knocked off if the model is handled without extreme care.

A Detail Associates rerail frog was hung below the walkway on the engineer's side of the locomotive using two short pieces of brass rod shaped like fish hooks. Holes were drilled into the bottom of the walkway and also through the white-metal rerail frog. The brass "fish hooks" were pressed into the holes in the locomotive and cemented in place with CA. Next, the rerail frog was fitted onto the hooks and it too was cemented in place.

We are almost done! Kadee® No. 8 couplers were fit to the coupler pockets provided and checked for operation and gauged for height. Railing ends were brush-painted yellow as were all grabirons and step edges. The rerail frog was painted red as was the antenna base and conduit. The under-the-walkway bell was painted brass.

At this point all that remained to do was weather the model and fit window glass. I first weathered the model so not to ruin the window glass. As always, I used an airbrush and Floquil paint thinned with automotive-quality lacquer thinner for weathering. And as usual, the model immediately was transformed from its toy-like appearance into one that is quite convincing. I cannot emphasize it enough — if you want realistic-appearing models, then weathering is the most important "detail" you can add. Without it, then... We've been down that road before, so I'll drop it there.

I don't care for the clear-plastic "glass" that comes with the model. It is a one-piece affair that fits flush with the inside of the cab and makes the cab walls look unrealistic because of the excessive recess of the windows. I cut individual window sections from .005 Evergreen clear sheet styrene and fit each in place. Microscale clear decal film was used to secure each in place. **I**

SAL 1405 is one of three S2s the SAL purchased in 1942. Hialeah, FL; May 17, 1964. *Warren Calloway collection, courtesy of* Diesel Era *magazine*

SAL 1429 is seen at Hialeah, FL, on April 27, 1963. *Warren Calloway collection, courtesy of* Diesel Era *magazine*

SAL 1431 at Hialeah, FL, on February 15, 1964. *Warren Calloway collection, courtesy of* Diesel Era *magazine*

Bill of Materials

Qty.	Manufacturer	Part No.	Description
1	Atlas		S2 locomotive (prepainted Seaboard)
1 set	Microscale	87-565	Seaboard Air Line switcher decals
1 set	Microscale	87-566	Seaboard Air Line yellow stripes
2	Kadee	8	Couplers
1 pkg.	Detail Associates	2202	Formed-wire drop-type grabs
1	Detail Associates	7103	Rerail frog
2	MV Products	136	12" headlight lenses

Union Pacific (UP) SW10
Rebuilt from EMD SW7, SW9 and TR5A Switchers

HO Scale Model by Athearn and Con-Cor
N Scale Model by Con-Cor

by Rich Picariello

Photos by the author

The Prototype SW10: Union Pacific rebuilt 75 SW7, SW9 and TR5A switchers into (UP) class SW10 locomotives at their Omaha Shops beginning in September 1979 and ending in December 1984. While UP supplied most of the locomotives used in this rebuilding program, some were former Missouri Pacific SW7 and Western Pacific SW9 units. The 1,200-hp rating of the original units remained unchanged, but the front-mounted radiator and its mechanical cooling fan were replaced with two 36″ electric fans and side-mounted radiator grilles salvaged from scrapped GP7s and GP9s. A raised sheet-metal housing was fabricated to accommodate these new components and a large sandbox was installed in place of the removed front radiator grille. All the SW10s ride on roller-bearing-equipped AAR switcher trucks.

The Scale Model SW10: HO scale SW7 models are available from Athearn and Con-Cor. Union Pacific SW10s have the square front cab windows as on Athearn's SW7 phase II model. Con-Cor's SW7 is the phase I version with arched front cab windows; the cab should be replaced with the listed Cannon phase II cab kit. A battery-access door will have to be added to each side of the cab (refer to part D). The most difficult part of the project will be the fabrication of the fan housing and the front sandbox. Roller-bearing truck sideframes (part #25) will easily replace the Athearn plain-bearing sideframes as they will press-fit into the trucks; the Con-Cor sideframes must be cut off and the new sideframes glued in their place. The front and rear pilot footboards on the Athearn or Con-Cor model must be removed.

N scale modelers can use a Con-Cor SW1500 (an improved version of the former Atlas SW1500) for their SW10 conversion. The angular cab roof on this model will have to be replaced with a new curved roof cut from sheet styrene.

Paint and Decal Notes: SW10s are painted in the standard UP yellow and gray with red stripes. Trucks, underframe, fuel tanks, pilots and walkways are gray; handrails are gray with white trim at the step areas. Window frames and all-weather windows (on units so equipped) are aluminum. Safety stripes for the pilots and the front and rear triangular panels are included on the Microscale HO and N scale decal sheets. All the listed scale models are available decorated for UP.

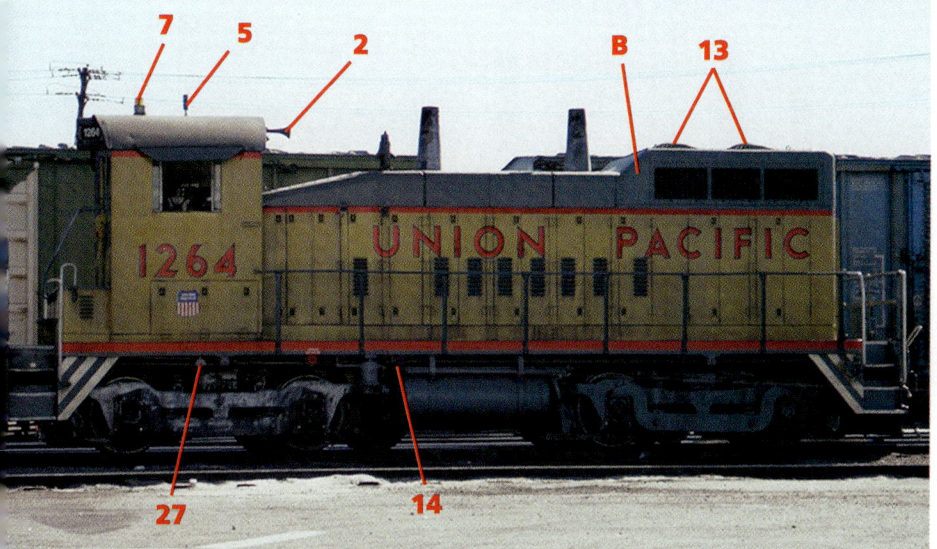

16
23
20
B
25
30
5
7
17
18
15
30
29
9
12
1268
UNION PACIFIC
22
E
C
3
1
D
27
10
11
21
19
F

25
4
8
20
20
23
20
9
1251
UNION PACIFIC
16
10
26
D
1
14
3
C
26

28
7
30
2
8
20
13
20
17
18
6
9
A
1270
UNION PACIFIC
15
27
14
3
19

Union Pacific SW10

Detail Parts for HO Scale:

#	Part	Description	Price
1 -	DW199	Air filter, Prime Type 2	1.25/ea.
2 -	CF219	Air horn (brass)	2.29/ea.
	CS423	Air horn (brass)	2.50/2
	DW174	Air horn (brass)	2.00/2
3 -	KS51	Air tank (metal, need 2)*	.95/ea.
4 -	DA2301	All-weather window (plastic)	1.50/2
	OM9716	All-weather window (brass)	1.95/ea.
	Note: On No. 1251 only.		
5 -	CF113	Antenna	3.09/2
	DW157	Antenna	1.50/6
6 -	DA2303	Armrest, cab	1.25/4
	Note: On No. 1270 only.		
7 -	DA2902	Beacon	1.50/2
	DW106	Beacon	1.00/ea.
	OM9101	Beacon	2.80/ea.
8 -	CS322	Bell (brass)	2.45/ea.
	DW128	Bell (metal)	1.25/2
9 -	DW132	Brake ratchet	1.00/ea.
10 -	CC1504	Cab, late-model EMD switchers*	8.50/kit
11 -	DA2211	Coupler lift bar	2.00/2
	OM9151	Coupler lift bar	1.95/2
12 -	OM9171	Door handle	1.67/2
13 -	DW142	Fan, 36″	1.25/4
	PSC3990	Fan, 36″ w/open ribs	2.25/4
14 -	DA3102	Fuel filler (plastic)†	1.00/set
	DW166	Fuel filler (metal)	1.00/4
	PSC39080	Fuel filler (plastic)	1.50/4
15 -	DA2202	Grabirons	2.50/48
16 -	SV23	Handrail set	15.95/ea.
	Note: SW1000/1500 handrail set, may have to be modified for the SW10.		
17 -	DA1011	Headlight	1.50/2
18 -	MV22	Headlight lenses	1.10/4
19 -	CS277	Hose, air line (brass)	2.15/4
	DA6206	Hose, air line (delrin)	1.25/6
20 -	DA2206	Lift rings	3.00/36
21 -	CF257	MU hoses, 3-per bracket (brass)	4.95/4
	DA1508	MU hoses, individual (delrin)	2.00/16
	OM9350	MU hoses, 3-per bracket (brass)	6.10/4
22 -	DA1507	MU receptacles & covers	1.25/30
23 -	DA2721	Radiator grille	2.95/2
24 -	DA3001	Sand-fill hatch (plastic)	1.25/6
	OM9400	Sand-fill hatch (brass)	3.30/2
25 -	AL29210	Sunshade (photo-etched brass)	1.95/6
	DA1301	Sunshade (plastic)	1.25/6
	DW188	Sunshade (plastic)	.80/4
	PSC39047	Sunshade (brass)	2.25/4
26 -	DA3501	Truck sideframes w/roller bearings	8.95/4
27 -	CF112	Underframe/step light (brass)	2.95/2
	DW172	Underframe/step light (metal)	1.25/8
28 -	DA2310	Wind deflector (clear plastic)	1.25/4
	UP77	Wind deflector/mirror (brass)	2.00/2
	Note: Not on all units, check photos.		
29 -	AMB231	Window glass (laser-cut plastic)*	3.95/set
	RUN1861	Window glass (vacu-formed plastic)*	2.00/set
	Note: The Cannon cab comes with a clear plastic sheet for glass.		
30 -	AL29200	Windshield wipers (delrin)	1.75/8
	CS419	Windshield wipers (brass)	3.50/4
	PSC3968	Windshield wipers (plastic)	1.50/4
	UP94	Windshield wipers (brass)	2.00/4
	UP97	Windshield wipers (plastic)	1.50/4

The following parts must be fabricated by the modeler:

A — Front sandbox — make from styrene.

B — Fan housing — build from styrene sheet.

C — Underframe piping — form from brass wire.

D — Battery-box doors — use the three-hinge doors from Cannon #1203 (SP "Split" Equipment Doors @ $2.95/6) or make from thin styrene sheet.

E — MU stands — make from styrene, add MU receptacle parts (see #21).

F — Lower pilot panels — make from styrene sheet.

G — ACI panel (on #1263 only) — make from thin brass.

* Similar parts, either separate or molded on, are included with the listed HO scale models; replacement of any or all original parts is left to the discretion of the modeler.

† DA3102 Fuel Tank Fittings (set) contains other parts that may or may not be needed for this detailing project.

AL/PPW: *A-Line/Proto Power West*
P.O. Box 7916
La Verne, CA 91750

AMB: *American Model Builders*
1420 Hanley Industrial Court
St. Louis, MO 63144

CS: *Cal-Scale*
21 Howard Street
Montoursville, PA 17754

CC: *Cannon and Company*
310 Willow Heights
Aptos, CA 95003

CF: *Custom Finishing*
379 Tully Road
Orange, MA 01364

DA: *Detail Associates*
Box 5357
San Luis Obispo, CA 93403

DW: *Details West*
P.O. Box 5132
Hacienda Heights, CA 91745

KS: *Keystone Locomotive Works*
P.O. Box J
Pulteny, NY 14874

MV: *MV Products*
P.O. Box 6622
Orange, CA 92667

OM: *Overland Models Inc.*
5908 W. Kilgore Avenue
Muncie, IN 47304

PSC: *Precision Scale Company*
3961 Hwy. 93 North
Stevensville, MT 59870

RUN: *Run 8 Productions*
P.O. Box 25224
Rochester, NY 14625

SV: *Smokey Valley Railroad Products*
P.O. Box 339
Plantersville, MS 38862

UP: *Utah Pacific*
9520 E. Napier Avenue
Benton Harbor, MI 49022

Note: These detail parts may be available at your local hobby dealer(s), so try there first. If you must order directly from a manufacturer, include at least **$3.50** for postage and handling. You must purchase the full quantities as shown in the detail parts list.

DECALS:

HO Scale:
Champion BRH-25
Herald King L-482
Microscale 87-373

N Scale:
Microscale 60-373

PAINTS:

Accu-flex:
16-02 Reefer White
16-24 UP Armour Yellow
16-25 UP Harbor Mist Gray

Accu+paint:
1   Stencil White

67	UP/Milw Armour Yellow
68	UP/Milw Harbor Mist Gray

Floquil:
110011 Reefer White
110166 UP Armour Yellow
110167 UP Harbor Mist Gray

Scalecoat:

11	White
22	UP Armour Yellow
32	UP Harbor Mist Gray

Scalecoat II (plastic compatible paint):

2011	White
2022	UP Armour Yellow
2032	UP Harbor Mist Gray

It is a matter of record that Southern 2526 and 2641, both GP30s, were so badly wrecked that they had to be sent back to EMD for rebuild. They were rebuilt, with a date of December 1965, and returned to the railroad. The interesting thing is that since EMD had completed the run of GP30s sometime before and was now building only GP35s these two engines were returned clad in GP35 bodies, although they still bore the GP30 designation.

This can lead one into all sorts of speculations. Consider the SD24. This was mechanically an SD30, since it had the same engine (Model 567D3) and main generator (Model D-22) as the GP30. Just suppose that one of the early SD24s, say CNO&TP 6306, had been so badly damaged in a wreck that it had to be sent to EMD for rebuilding. Further, suppose that this happened in August or September 1963. By then the last SD24 had long been finished, and as EMD was prone to do, the body dies had been scrapped. The only engines then in production were the GP30s. So what would EMD do for a body for the rebuild? It seems logical that the GP30 parts on hand could be stretched out to fit the SD24 mechanicals, and we would have an SD30. So with this scenario as a rationale, here is how one can build a model of this most peculiar engine.

Although I had thought about building one of these for a long time, it was a conversation with Dean Freytag at his house that finally prompted me to go ahead with the model. Some of you may remember the low-nose SD30 built by Dean and the late Ray Miller that took the Kitbashing Award in *Railroad Model Craftsman* in April 1987. We were looking at the engine and Dean said that he would sure like to see a high-nose Southern version of the beast — so when I got home I began to collect the parts.

The body shell was made from two of the old Bachmann GP30 shells. Dean and Ray had used an Atlas SD24/SD35 chassis, but since I did not have one of these to spare, I used an Athearn SD9 frame and trucks with a Mashima motor and A-line flywheels since this would provide the proper truck centers and C-C trucks. This frame requires radical surgery, but it is not all that difficult.

Major SD30 Modification

The first step is to cut the two shells. Cut the first one just behind the seventh tall door; cut the second shell just behind the third tall door, leaving about 6³/₄ tall doors on the radiator/fan end of the shell which we will be using. See Photos 1 & 2.

Now the frame can be modified. First file off the four cast-on body-mounting lugs. Next, fit the cab end of the shell over the end of the frame which has the part numbers cast in the top. The angled ends of the frame should fit up against the back of the steps. Mark the two sides of the frame where the shell is recessed for the battery boxes. Note that this is different on each side. Cut the frame on these two marks, so that the frame will fit into the cab end of the shell with the bottom of the frame even with the raised part of the sidesill. Remove the cab half of the shell and fit the radiator end in the same manner. On this end both frame sides are cut at the same location to fit inside the raised part of the walkway (air duct). This will place the marks, and the cuts, about ³/₃₂″ behind the bolster. (The cab end of the engine will be the front.) The vertical legs of the bolster will have to be filed to fit inside the narrow hood of the GP30 shell. File them back so that the outside of the legs are even with the opening in the frame, then file off the raised lip that runs from the bolster to the motor recess.

by Jim Teese, MMR / Photos by the author unless otherwise indicated

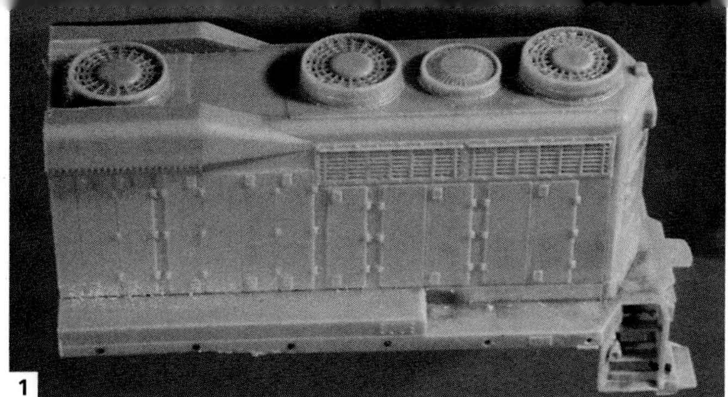

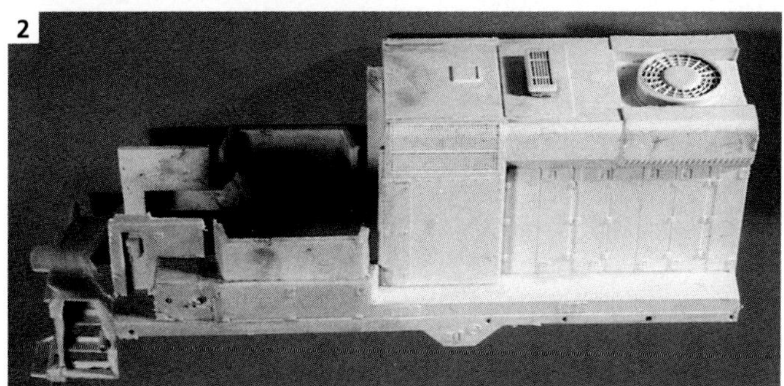

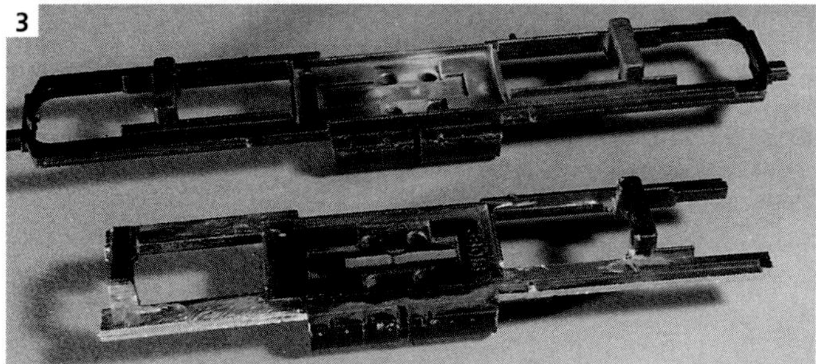

This must be done on both ends of the frame. Photo 3 shows the modified frame next to an unmodified one.

Trim the wide (thick) part of the sidesill on the radiator end of the shell to the same thickness as the thinner section of the sidesill, roughly $\frac{1}{16}''$. This will allow both ends of the shell to sit well down on the frame, with the bottom of the frame even with the raised portion of the sidesill. See Photo 4.

High Short Hood

I haven't seen a discussion of the peculiarities of the GP30's high short hoods in any published modeling articles. For one thing, the distinctive over-the-top ducting (eyebrows?) on the high short hood does not go as far forward as it does on the low-hood version (see prototype photos on page 30). It must be shortened about 18″ so the front 18″ of the cab roof must be formed as part of the top of the short hood. After building several of the high short hood GP30s it has become evident that the easiest and best way is to construct the hood from several pieces. Cut the front of the existing short hood off at the mold parting line, then cut off the sides as high as possible to save the cast-on catches for the battery-box lids on both sides. This also enables the molded brake assembly to be saved. See Photo 2 again.

Now cement the cab in place, filing as required to ensure a good fit. After this has thoroughly dried, the two halves of the shell can be filed to fit together, using the frame to ensure that everything lines up properly. The joint across the top of the fitted shell should come

halfway between the two dynamic-brake fans. When satisfied with the fit, cement the two halves of the shell together, on the frame, and allow to dry thoroughly. Apply a reinforcing piece of .040 styrene only on the inside of the top — there is no room for reinforcement on the sides or walkways.

Cut the tall hood end from the discarded section of the first shell, cutting along the mold parting lines. Fit this to the remaining part of the short hood sides and the front section of the walkway. The ducting on the cab roof should be cut back about 24″, with the cuts parallel to the slope of the original front of the ducting, above the numberboards. See Photo 5.

Now cement the new front end of the hood to the remaining part of the sides. Make sure that it is lined up on the centerline and that it is vertical. See Photo 6.

Cut two pieces of .060 styrene to make the top part of the short hood sides. File the front of the cab so these pieces fit inside the cab front walls. When satisfied with the fit, cement in place. After the hood sides have dried, scribe a line on both sides and the end about .080 below and parallel with the top of the cab. Cut and file the assembly to this line, then file the opening in the cab roof so that it is the same width as the outside of the hood sides. See Photo 7.

Cut a piece of .080 styrene the width of the hood and long enough so that it projects inside the cab roof under the cut ducting. The front of this piece should be trimmed to match the hood end and cemented in place. It may help to use rubber bands (with the shell mounted on the frame) to ensure that it is tight. See Photo 8.

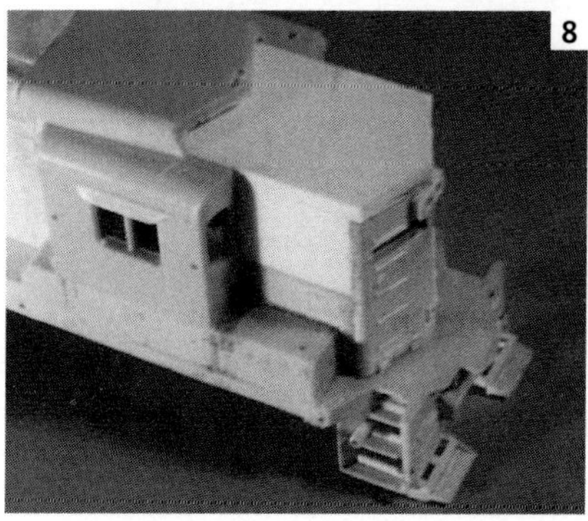

When dry it is time to shape the top corners of the hood. It is inevitable that the top molded grab will be removed during this shaping. Mark the center of the two bumps representing the grab fasteners and drill #76. Use care in shaping the joint between the top hood corner and the cab front — I had to use putty on both sides to get it right. Now the new front for the duct may be installed. Cut two pieces of .060 styrene with the bottoms and the center edges filed to the proper angle and cement in place. They will be trimmed later. See Photo 9.

9

This is a good time to do the final surgery on the shell. First, to digress. At this time a decision must be made as to the style of fuel tank to be used. The easiest would be to use the tank as cast on the Athearn frame. Alternatively, the tank can be reshaped to the same style as the GP30 (and the SD35). The triangular panel on the sidesill that extends down with the GP30 fuel filler must be removed regardless, since it will interfere with the longer truck. The best way to do this is to saw it off even with the bottom of the sill and file off the portion of the molded filler that remains on the sidesill. If the decision is to go with the stock frame the fuel-filler panel need not be replaced, since the cast-on tank has integral fuel fillers. If you do decide on this style, you may re-detail the tank to suit your fancy. I elected to re-style the tank to the more modern design. This entails milling off about 18″ of the top part of the tank on each side. If you do not have access to a vertical mill a Dremel will do the job just about as well. See Photo 10.

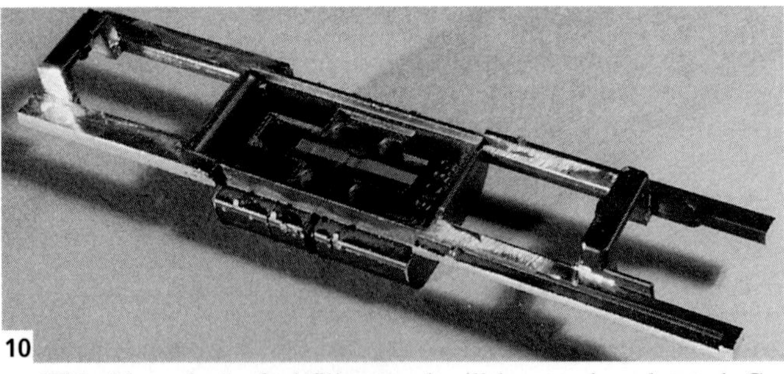

10

With this tank the fuel-filler panel will have to be relocated. Cut the ones from the scrap shell, sawing from each end of the angle up to the division line in the sill. Cut off and file the panel top even with this line. Then notch the sidesill to fit so that the front of the panel is even with the front of the tank and cement the panel in place. See Photo 11.

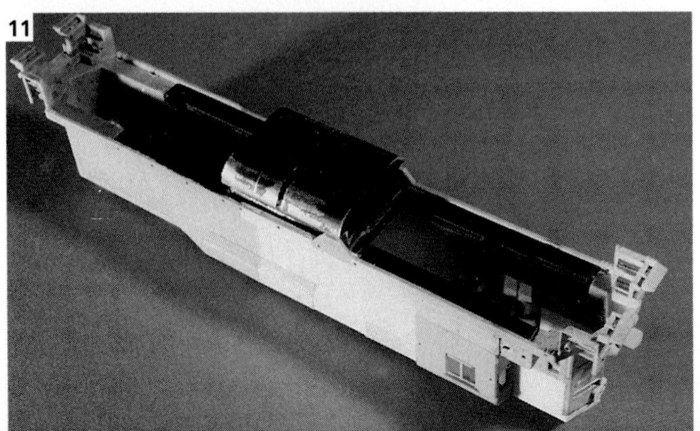

11

12

Next is the removal of the grabs and classification lights from both ends. Mark the location of the grab fasteners as described above, and drill #76. The center of the class lights should also be located the same way. Now trim off the grabs, class lights and the molded gaskets around the numberboards from both ends and smooth. Also trim the front of the duct and begin to apply putty as required. See Photo 12.

In addition to the grabs cast on the original shell there is a straight grab on the top at both ends, as well as the curved grab just behind the rear fan. Locate the ends of these three grabs and drill #76. Now cement DA2203 NBWs in the #76 holes drilled for the grab fasteners on both ends of the shell. The hole marked for the center of the class lights should be drilled #42 and DA1019 class lights installed. See Photo 13.

13

When the NBWs have thoroughly dried drill #79 for the Westerfield 1198 grabs. The long grab and curved grab on the rear are bent from DA2504 .012 brass wire. Install all the grabs with CA except the bottom ones on each end. These will be installed after the engine is painted and decaled. Photo 14 shows the grabs in place on the rear of the engine.

Drill #60 in the center of the cab roof and CA the DW187 Nathan M5 air horn in place. Then mount the DW135 bell on the high short hood with CA. Note that it is immediately adjacent to the NBW forming the inside fastener for the top grab. Fill the handrail holes in the cab sides, the inside of the steps and the bottom of the pilots with the ends of the original handrails and smooth.

14

I have never been happy with the brass firecracker antennae available in HO. Seems that they bend and break off with a hard look! So the following method provides an alternative. Cement the small square blank cover from the DA1506 MU-stand package in the location desired as the antenna base. In this case it is centered on the short hood halfway between the back of the bell bracket and the front of the duct. See Photo 15.

When thoroughly dry, drill #77 and CA a short piece of K&S 498 .015 music wire in the hole so that it projects 12″ above the base. Drill #67 for the three

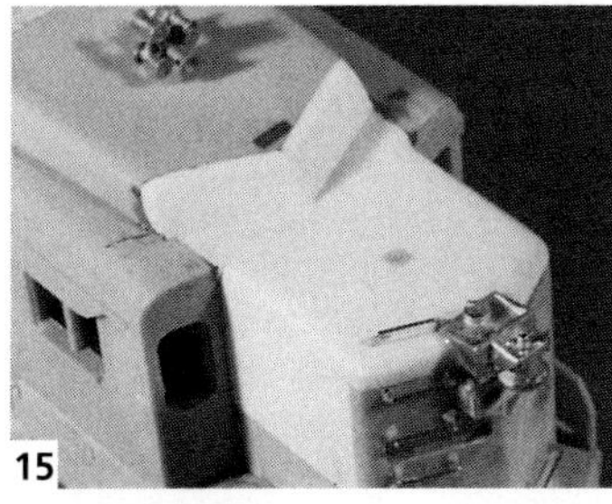

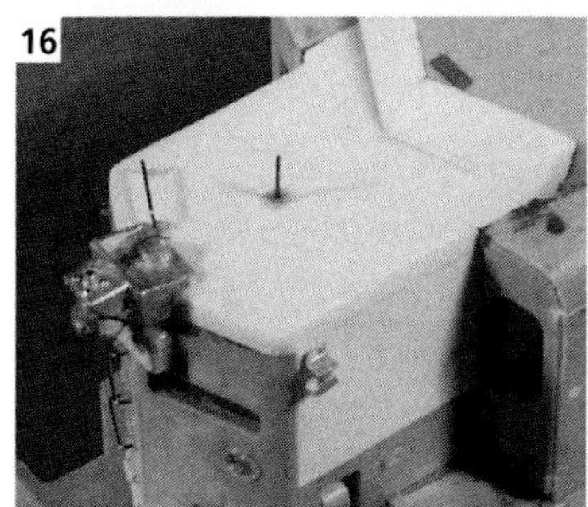

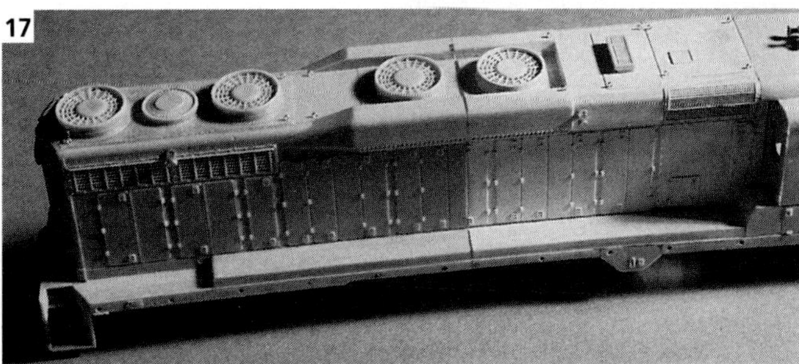

OMI 9708 walkway lights and install with CA. Also cement the battery-box cover plate on the left side of the engine ahead of the cab. Drill #80 and mount the 14 DA2206 lift rings with CA. Cement a DA3001 sand-filler hatch on the top center of the long hood end, and cement the supplied GP30 exhaust stack in place. See Photos 16,17 & 18.

The final step in the construction of the "unbreakable" antenna is to cut a short piece of insulation from the Brawa 3168 flex wire. Trim to a length of 8″ with the ends square and CA to the .015 music wire with the top flush. Voila! See Photo 19.

This is a good time to airbrush a coat of SP Lark Light Gray on the shell to check for defects. While the paint dries we'll work on the chassis.

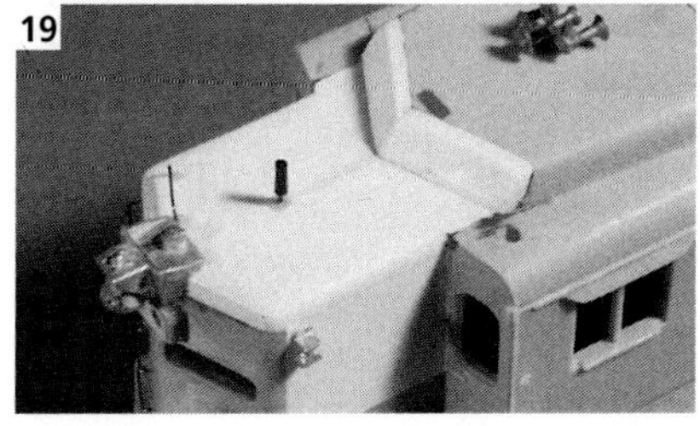

Fuel Tank

An appropriate fuel tank for this model can be constructed of sheet styrene, using .060 styrene for the ends and a wrap of .020 styrene for the sides and bottom. If you are lucky, however, you may

be able to locate a GSB 40-2-1007 tank. This is the tank used on their SD40-2, and is the perfect tank for any of the earlier SD series. Another possible tank would be the Smokey Valley 62, the fuel tank made for

their GP15, but I do not know if it is too long or too short. Back to the GSB tank. Assemble it, then cut off and discard the end without the air tanks, leaving the end with the air tanks 14′ 6″ long. Cut off the two air tanks and save, as shown in Photo 20.

File and sand the fuel-tank casting smooth and fit it to the frame, filing as necessary to properly adjust. When satisfied, fasten it to the frame with silicone sealant and allow to cure. While curing, inspect the shell for defects and putty as required. See Photo 21.

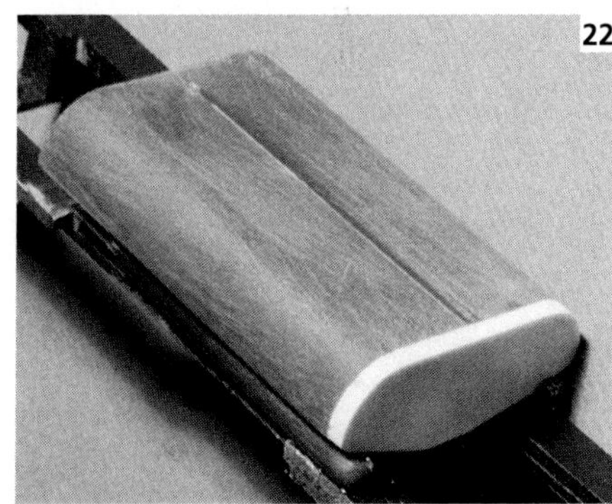

Cut a piece of .080 styrene for the end of the tank and cement in place. When dry apply putty as necessary and smooth. Trim the two air tanks and round their ends, then CA in place with the ends of the air tanks projecting about .060 beyond the new fuel tank end. See Photo 22.

The Athearn trucks should be run-in with Pearl Drops tooth polish (from your local drug store) on the gears for about 30 minutes in each direction, then disassembled, washed and dried. Be careful not to wash one of the small gears down the drain as I did! Replace the Athearn wheels with NWSL 71424 wheels to improve looks and performance and replace the original sideframes with DA3514 sideframes with low brake cylinders, since these were the trucks used on the Southern SD35s and seemed appropriate for the SD30. If you have ever looked closely at an engine that has been in use for some time you will see that the wheels and sideframes are the same color. Before reassembling the trucks, airbrush the sideframes and the wheels with Pactra M1 and then dust on your light weathering color. (My preference is Floquil Antique White.) At the same time airbrush the frame — being sure to mask the contact area on the bolster. Mount the A-Line 20006 flywheels on the Mashima motor and then mount it temporarily to the frame with double-stick foam tape. Assemble the trucks to the frame and hard wire with the Brawa 3168 flex wire as shown in Photo 23. Test run and fix any problems.

Fabricate the coupler mounts from three layers of .060 styrene, drill #51 and tap 2-56 for the coupler mounting screws. Make up a pair of Kadee® #5 couplers and cut the ears off the boxes. Notice that I cut off the trip pin on my couplers since my railroad does not use magnetic uncoupling. The couplers should be mounted with the front of the box just inside the slanted part of the pilot. This will enable them to swing properly and still not project unrealistically far. Mount the shell on the frame and check coupler height with the Kadee gauge. Adjust as necessary with shims or by filing. The mounts are shown in Photo 24.

Another peculiarity of Southern's high short hood engines is the awning with its integral rain gutter. Look carefully at the prototype photos and it becomes apparent that the awning has an upward curl at the outer edge — like the old handle-bar mustache! The only satisfactory way I have found to model these is to use a piece of K&S 171 ⅛" x ⅛" brass angle and file (or grind with a Dremel tool) one of the legs off, down just past the beginning of the curve. Smooth the cut, rounding

it off upward and cut the awning to length. Fasten to the cab with CA. Photo 25 shows the shaped angle, with one of the awnings cut off and mounted on the cab and the other still attached, ready to cut off. This photo also shows the #52 hole drilled for the fuel filler.

The opening in the center of the pilot should be filled in with four thicknesses of .040 styrene, the first across the back of the pilot as a base, then the next as the extension of the pilot proper and the final two as the center of the MU-hose end box. It is a good idea to mount the coupler box while doing this to make sure of clearances. See Photo 26.

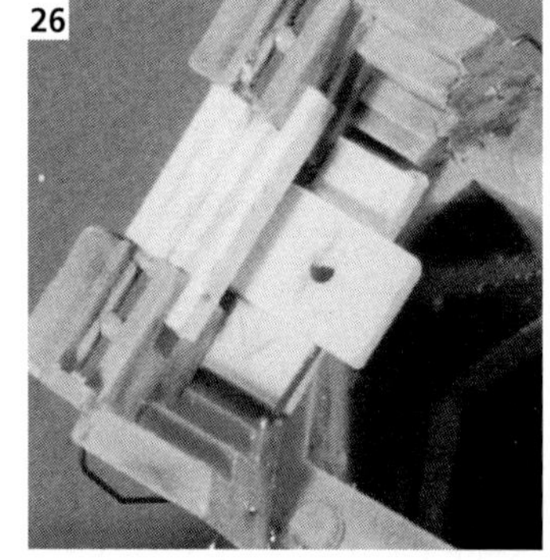

The handrails are fabricated from K&S 498 .015 music wire and Athearn stanchions of all three sizes. With one exception the handrails are the same as those on the GP30. The long side handrails must be lengthened to make up for the longer hood, and one new stanchion hole must be drilled on each side. At the joint of the two main shell pieces you will wind up with two stanchion holes about 16" apart. Fill these two holes and drill the new one #61 centered between them. The new railing holes in the cab, step wells and pilots should be drilled #77. CA the handrails in place securely, then add the DA1401 drop steps and the DA1506 MU stands to each end. Cut off the slanted base on the MU stands and mount

them on their sides to replicate the arrangement Southern used on their engines during this period. This photo also shows the recess drilled into the center of the DA class lights to hold the white jewels used to simulate illuminated lights. To me the sparkle of jewels is preferable to the MV lenses, but do whichever you prefer. See Photo 27.

Have you ever taken a good look at the chain that hangs between the two handrails on the ends of a locomotive (or for that matter, a caboose)? The prototype is a chain with links about ½" to ⅝" OD — equivalent to about .005 in HO. The smallest chain available to my knowledge is 40 links to the inch, with an OD of .035. This scales out to about 3¼"

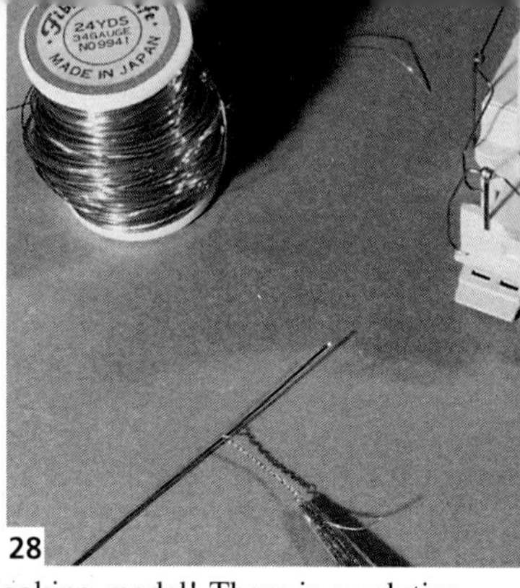

— somewhat too large for a good looking model! There is a solution, however. Pick up a roll of Fibre-Craft "bead wire" at your local craft shop. This is a hard brass 34 gauge wire — about .006 in diameter. Cut a piece about 2" long and form a tight U in the center. Put this U around the handrail, cross the ends and hold them with a hemostat as shown. Pulling the wire up against the handrail, twist tightly to form an even spiral. Then back off slightly to open the spiral just a tad. You will now have something that looks like a very small chain — actual diameter about .012, or a scale 1". This is still a bit oversized, but to me it is preferable to the appearance of the 40-link chain. Open the "chain" back to the length desired and use the ends of wire to mount the other end. CA in place. See Photo 28.

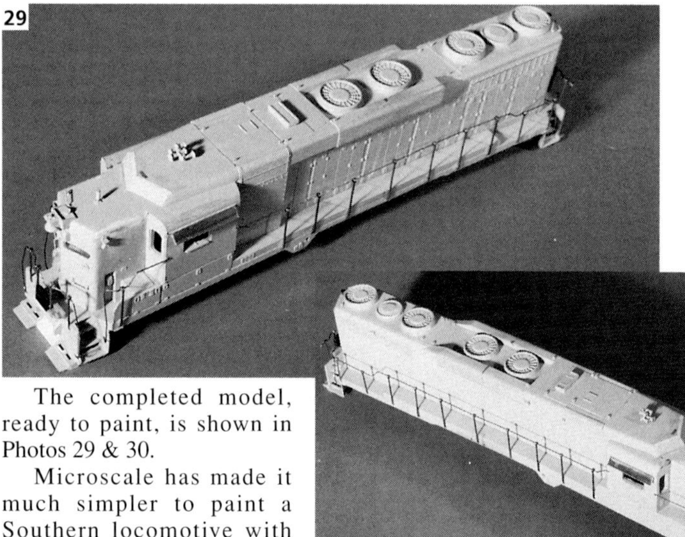

The completed model, ready to paint, is shown in Photos 29 & 30.

Microscale has made it much simpler to paint a Southern locomotive with their introduction of the gray and gold stripes (87-540) to compliment their original 87-32, the gold Southern hood unit set. However, the step and pilot footboard edge stripes, as well as the striping to cover the step where the duct ends on the side walkways can only be found on 87-539. So you will need all three decal sets. Now what is needed is a good coat of black paint. For this model Floquil Military Black was used. This paint has a very finely ground pigment which produces an extremely smooth semi-gloss finish that is suitable for decals without a gloss coating. Before applying the paint cement the numberboards in place on both ends. Since the numberboards are the same color as the shell it is it is easier to do it this way. Airbrush several light coats over the shell, making sure to get good coverage on those areas where the paint is subject to being rubbed off, such as the upper ends of the handrail stanchions, the outside of the awnings, the lift rings and other projections. When the paint has dried thoroughly begin the decal process with the stripes. Be sure to follow the directions on the decal package — it takes several applications of Micro Sol to adhere the stripe over all the hinges and latches on the hood sides, but it can be done. After the striping is complete, add the roadname and numbers, end heralds and the small lettering such as the "600 volts" on red panels from 87-527, builders plate from MC-4056 and the "fuel" over the fuel filler from 87-539.

The most difficult part of the decal job is the zebra stripes on the pilots. The only way I have ever been able to get a decent job is to apply them one stripe at a time, seal tight with Micro Sol and then apply the

next one.
It is time con-
suming, but it works.
The white striping on the step
and footboard edges is the final
touch. Using a good detergent and a soft
brush clean all the solvent marks off the shell and
airbrush the entire model with Dullcote. Now the pilot
detail can be added — .015 wire handrails, coupler lift bars, MU
hoses (four on each side at each end in #74 holes) and the CalScale
277 brake hose at each end mounted in #66 holes. To prevent smear-
ing the striped pilots it is best to prepaint all these items before
CA'ing them in place. Also install the three lower grabs in the gray
stripe, prepainted black, that were not installed before painting.

This is a good time to re-install the Kadee #5 couplers. Again flying
in the face of much learned opinion my observation has been that locomotive couplers take on the same colors as the rest of the pilot as a result
of weathering. This technique provides that coloration. Airbrush again
with Dullcote, and then start to weather. The shell was first dusted with
the light weathering, enough to show that the engine had been working
but not enough to obscure the detail. Then it was placed on the chassis
and the entire model was given a nice greenish grime, a little heavier on
the pilots, steps and chassis. Next install the Sequoia 5005 clear jewels in
the class lights with CA and the windshields of Evergreen 9005 clear
styrene fastened with white glue. The advantage of white glue here is that
it dries transparent and will not mark either the shell or the windshield.
A-Line long windshield wipers were painted and installed in #77 holes.
The shell is now complete. See Photos 31 & 32.

Directional Lighting

Diode-controlled directional headlights are a requirement on all my
diesel locos. Before installing them it is best to mount the motor permanently with silicone. Remove the double-stick tape and clean the
bottom of the motor and the frame where the motor will mount.
Because of the narrow shell it is essential that the motor be lined up
correctly. A simple method of doing this is to squeeze a small amount
of the silicone on the frame, then place the motor in the approximate
position. Cover the motor and the frame with a couple thicknesses of

heavy
clear plastic
(vinyl) and press the
shell down on the frame all
the way. When the silicone has
cured, the motor will be properly aligned.

Because of the limited space available in this
shell it was decided to construct a lighting module
using the smallest available parts. The Deans two-pin connector should be available at any hobby shop catering to radio-con-
trolled airplanes. The big advantage to this connector is that if one
goofs, and the headlights come on in the wrong direction, a simple
inverting of the male section of the connector will cure the trouble. Solder the wires from the trucks to one pin of the female half of the connector and a wire from the other pin to the top brush of the motor.
Mount this half of the connector on the end of the motor as shown,
using silicone to hold it in place. The electronics are very simple — six
1 amp diodes (such as the Radio Shack 276-1101 used here) mounted
on a small piece of Perfboard. Photo 33 shows how they are mounted
(on a sparc bit of Perfboard) and how the wiring is connected. The
bulbs are Miniatronics 18-CO3-10.

Fasten the Perfboard to the inside of the cab roof with silicone,
then insert the bulbs in the headlights and use a small amount of
white glue to secure them. See Photo 34.

Put an engineer in the cab and inspect the model carefully. Correct
any mistakes and put the model on the railroad. Enjoy! My SD30 was
placed in service on 16 January 1995.

SR 2630, Asheville, NC; June 25, 1986

J. E. Parker photo

SR 2630, Asheville, NC; June 25, 1986

J. E. Parker photo

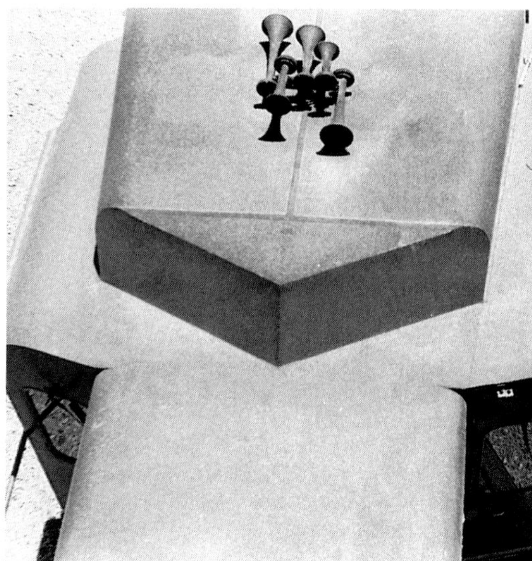

SR 2630, Asheville, NC; June 25, 1986

J. E. Parker photo

BILL OF MATERIALS

Manufacturer	Part No.	Description
A-line	20006	Flywheels
	29200	Windshield wipers
Athearn		SD9 powered chassis
	10424	Handrail stanchions
	10425	Handrail stanchions
	10426	Handrail stanchions
	99002	2-56 x $^1/_4$" screws
Bachmann		GP30 body shell (two)
Brawa	3168	Flex wire
CalScale	277	Hose — brass
Deans		Connector — see text
Detail Associates		
	1019	Class lights
	1401	Drop steps
	1506	MU-cable stands
	1508	MU air hoses
	2203	NBW
	2205	Coupler lift bars
	2206	Eyebolts (lift rings)
	2504	.012 brass wire
	2505	.015 brass wire
	3001	Sand-filler hatch
	3514	Sideframes
Details West	135	SRR/N&W high short hood bell
	187	Nathan M5 air horn
Evergreen	9005	.005 clear styrene
	9040	.040 white styrene
	9060	.060 white styrene
	9080	.080 white styrene
Floquil	303010	Military Black
	110131	SP Lark Light Gray
GSB	40-2-1007	Fuel tank — see text
Kadee®	5	Couplers
K&S	171	$^1/_8$" x $^1/_8$" brass angle
	498	.015 music wire
Mashima	1836	Flat can motor
Microscale	87-32	SRR Hood Diesels — Gold
	87-527	Loco Data and Late Builder's Plates
	87-539	SRR Hood Diesels — Dulux Gold
	87-540	SRR Gray and Gold Stripes
	MC-4056	Early Builder's Plates
Miniatronics		
	18-CO3-10	1.5V micro-miniature bulbs
NWSL	71424	Wheels
Overland	OMI 9708	Walkway lights
Pactra	M1	Scale Black
Radio Shack		
	276-1101	Miniature diodes
Sequoia	5005	Clear jewels
Testors		Dullcote
Westerfield	1198	18" straight grabs
Miscellaneous		Bead wire
		White glue
		Silicone sealant
		Putty
		CA
		Styrene cement
		Weathering paint
		Perfboard
		Pearl Drops tooth polish

SR 2531, Nixon, GA; December 1988   *J. W. Parker photo*

SR 2535, Augusta, GA; October 26, 1969   *J. E. Parker photo*

SR 2537, Aiken, SC; July 21, 1979
J. E. Parker photo

SR 2532, Warrenville, SC; October 1982
J. W. Parker photo

E8s 930, 929B and another E8A lead train #10 into the Hermosa Tunnel cut on May 13, 1951.   *R. H. Kindig photo, A. J. Wolff collection*

Modeling Union Pacific E8/9 Locomotives

KITBASHING PROTO 2000 B UNITS

by Randy Lee

Photos by the author unless otherwise indicated
Illustration by Rachael Amos

Union Pacific was a major user of E8s and E9s — both A and B units — and no UP modeler who models between 1950 and 1971 (when Amtrak took over passenger service) should be without some of these beautiful EMD passenger units. But even if you model a more recent period you can still justify having at least one. Present-day modelers can delight in the fact the UP had 949, 963B and 951 rebuilt in Paducah, KY, and returned on April 26, 1993.

Up until now, the only plastic E units available have been Con-Cor's E7A and Rivarossi's E8/9A and B (although Rivarossi's A units are readily available, their B units are difficult to find). Life-Like's latest Proto 2000 offering provides another choice. Their model is without question the nicest ready-to-run A unit ever produced. Life-Like offers it either as UP's E8A 926 or 928. These units look great and perform incredibly right out of the box without any modifications. Many modelers will choose to use them just as they come, and no apologies are necessary for those who do, because these are beautifully detailed models.

This article is intended for those modelers who want to do a little more detailing to make their A units more prototypically accurate for a particular time period or who want to kitbash a B unit or two. Life-Like has chosen to offer their UP E units as two E8s from UP's first order in 1950. The models feature dual steam generators and the original paint scheme with the Armour Yellow and the red stripes wrapping around the rear of the engine. These features are generally correct for E8s up through the mid-'50s.

The only "serious" missing detail on Life-Like's factory-painted UP models is the 36″ dynamic-brake fan found on 926-930 (all others had 48″ dynamic-brake fans [DW 143]). Other detail differences are relatively minor, but their addition (or deletion) is easy to do and will add to the accuracy of the model.

Although E8s and E9s are virtually identical externally, there are a couple of differences worth mentioning. First, all UP E8s had two headlight openings with recessed glass while most UP E9s had a single headlight opening with flush-mounted glass (900-909 had two flush-mounted headlight openings). Second, E8s originally had the early-style (some received late-style later) cab sand-fill hatches with round handles (DA 3003) while the E9s had the late-style hatch with a rectangular recess

This June 5, 1954, photo taken in Denver, CO, shows E9A 944 (and E8B 941B) in its as-delivered configuration, with yellow end, gray trucks, nose coupler door and no snow shields. Note single headlight. Third unit appears to be an E7.

R. H. Kindig photo, A. J. Wolff collection

UP 938B can be identified as an E8B because of its sand-fill hatches with round handles. Council Bluffs, IA; June 2, 1962.

L. Schmitz photo, A. J. Wolff collection

(DA 3004). The Life-Like model has the late-style hatch correct for an E9. You'll have to be the judge on whether you should replace them with correct ones. The third major visible difference between the UP's as-delivered E8As and E9As is that the E8As had dual 2,500 lbs./hr. steam generators and the E9As had a single 4,000 lbs./hr. steam generator. All B units had the single 4,000 lbs./hr. generator.

Early UP E8s (926-930, 926B-930B) had the horizontal grilles while later E8s (925, 931-942, 922B-925B, 931B-949B) and all E9s had the Farr vertical grilles. From the photographic evidence available to me, it appears that none of the UP's E8s and E9s had the grabirons going up the rear of the unit in ladder fashion as is found on the model. They instead had ladder-support grabs on each corner of the roof (and nose).

Visible Changes Over the Years

▼ Snow Shields and Paint — Beginning in the 1955-'56 time frame, UP added their distinctive "snow shields" to their E8s and E9s and began to paint the ends of the units Harbor Mist Gray and the trucks silver. Photos from this period show lashups where some units have gray ends and others yellow, some with and some without snow shields. The cover photo on the spring 1976 issue of *Great World of Model Railroading* (*MRG*'s predecessor) clearly shows unit 957B still with yellow ends in a 1959 or later photo. If you are modeling the mid-'50s you can mix these features as you please, but if you are doing the late '50s or later, all units should have snow shields.

▼ Steam Generators — Most of the dual 2,500 lbs./hr. steam generators in the E8As were eventually replaced with single 4,000 lbs./hr. generators. Most of these changes appear to have occurred in the '50s, but you should refer to specific unit photos if possible.

▼ Horns — So far I have been unable to find any UP units with a horn arrangement like the one found on the Life-Like model. For this detail item you are definitely going to have to rely on photos of the specific model you are building. The E8As delivered in 1950 were equipped with two separate single blat-type horns (DW 173). It gets more confusing after that. Take UP 930 for example. In 1951, it still had the two blat-type horns, but a 1953 photo shows it with the blat horn on the engineer's side replaced with a five-chime horn (OMI 9003 or CS 316) while the other rear-facing blat horn was still present. A 1963 photo of 930 shows it with both the original blat-type horns back in place again.

Most 1950s and early-'60s photos of later E8As and E9s show a forward-facing two-chime horn (OMI 9015) on the engineer's side and a rear-facing single blat on the fireman's side. An exception to this though is UP 937, which had two single blats in a 1961 Kindig photo. Check the photos here and in Gary Binder's excellent article, "Union Pacific Racehorses — E8 and E9 Diesels" in *The Streamliner*, Vol. 2., No. 2. It is still

This close-up view of the cab of E9A 944 clearly shows the air line for the horns going from the cab over the winterization hatch to the air-horn bracket. Cheyenne, WY; May 26, 1968.
A. J. Wolff photo

Note backup light and conduit on E9B 901B. Life-Like's model has a square door window rather than a round one, a relatively minor mistake considering that it will rarely be seen. Laramie, WY; June 21, 1968.
A. J. Wolff photo

UP E9A 945 was built in 1954 and featured EMD's "E9" designation plate (only 943 to 962 had these). Note box cover over boiler-water fill. Cheyenne, WY; September 21, 1969.
A. J. Wolff photo

ets and seam line on the roof. If this cut is carefully made, the cab with door frame can be preserved for some other project. With the furring-strip supports spaced about an ⅛" apart, the shell was laid on its side in X-Acto's large mitre box with the ladders against the closest wall; it just fits.

After carefully positioning the shell and saw, enough hand pressure was applied to keep the shell in place without risking breaking the ladders. After checking and rechecking, the cut was made through the side wall and about halfway through the roof. The shell was then turned over and the remainder of the cut was made from the other side. Again, measure carefully before cutting. The cuts must be straight, perpendicular to the shell and must come together smoothly in the center.

Once the cut has been completed and you've started breathing again, remove the furring-strip supports and insert them in the rear of the second shell. The cut on the second shell will be made just in front of the rivet strip on the car's side. This means the cut will obliterate the rivets on the roof because the seam line is where we want the edge of the cut to be. BE SURE THE CUT LEAVES THE SIDE'S RIVET STRIP ON THE

Table 1 — Railroads Rostering E8B and E9B Locomotives

(Table compiled from E8/E9 roster data presented by Dan Dover in the November/December 1973 issue of *Extra 2200 South*.)

Road	Model	Qty.	Dynamic Nos.	Brakes	Comments
Amtrak	E8B	5	370-374	Yes	Former UP units
	E9B	23	450-472	Yes	Former UP (18) and MILW (5) units
ATSF (Santa Fe)	E8B	5	80A - 84A	No	81A originally 4A
Atlantic Coast Line	E8B	2	765, 766	No	Became SCL 670B, 671A
Baltimore & Ohio	E8B	6	51x-56x	No	Renumbered 2414-2419
Illinois Central	E8B	2	4104, 4105	No	ICG 2100, 2101
	E9B	4	4106-4109	No	ICG 2102-2105
Milwaukee Road	E9B	6	200B-205B	Yes	Renumbered 30B-35B
Richmond, Fredericksburg & Potomac (RF&P)	E8B	5	1051-1055	No	1054, 1055 became ACL 765, 766
Rock Island	E8B	8	613-620	No*	Former UP units, acquired summer 1968
Union Pacific	E8B	28	922B-949B	Yes	
	E9B	34	900B-904B, 910B-913B, 950B-974B	Yes	

*Although these are former UP units which were equipped with dynamic brakes, Mr. Dover's roster shows them without dynamic brakes on the Rock Island.

All B units were originally equipped with single 4,000 lbs./hr. steam generators except ATSF (two 2,250), B&O (two 2,880) and MILW (two 2,500).

END PIECE BEING CUT OFF. If you haven't already realized it, we are going to hide our seam on the edge of the rivet strip on the sides and along the natural seam line on the roof. This means the only sections of the seam which aren't "hidden" are along the bottom horizontal rivet strip and the short distance on the curve between the sides and the top panel's seam. Once again, cut through the side wall and halfway through the roof and then finish the cut from the other side.

2 – With the cuts complete, and after you're finished speculating about freelancing a doubled-ended A unit, it's time to prepare the cuts so the two sections can be attached to form the B unit. How carefully the cuts were made will determine the amount of sanding that will be necessary. If zero-tolerance cuts were made, all that will be necessary is to smooth the surfaces so a smooth, solid joint can be made. If your cuts weren't quite perfectly perpendicular or weren't right against either the panel line on the first shell or the rivet strip on the second shell, a little more sanding may be required. I required a "little more" sanding.

A few words of caution about sanding. Again, be sure to use a fur-ring-strip support inside the shell near the cut. Place the sandpaper on a flat surface and move the shell on the sandpaper. Don't use too coarse a paper; go slowly and test fit regularly. Remember too that there will be a natural tendency for more to be sanded off the bottom than by the roof simply because there is so much more material around the roof. If you're not careful, this will result in the end sloping down when the pieces are glued together. Once again, I speak from experience.

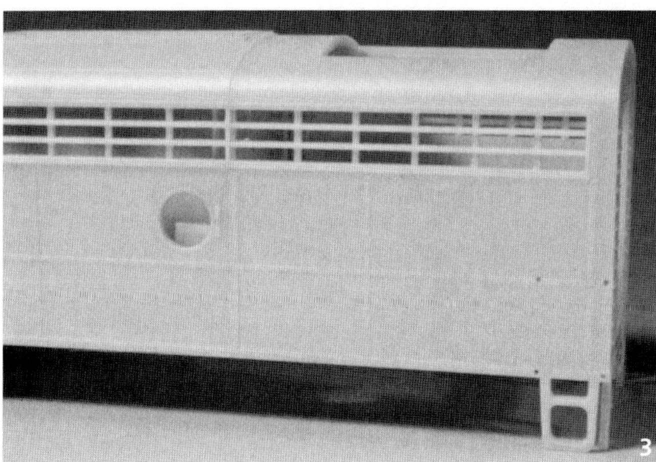

3 – After the sanding is complete, test fit the pieces together to make sure there are no visible gaps and that the horizontal lines continue on straight past the joint when viewed down the length of the shell. When you are satisfied, it's time to glue the pieces together. I carefully laid the two pieces on my project board, making sure that the bottoms were aligned, and applied a liberal amount of Tenax 7R to the inside of the wall joint while applying firm pressure, forcing the two pieces together. After allowing the solvent to work for about a minute, I carefully lifted the shell, being careful to keep it together as one, and laid it down on the other side and repeated the process for the other wall. After making minor adjustments while the joints were still flexible I applied the solvent

to the inside of the roof, rechecked everything again and then allowed the cemented joint to cure. A periodic check to make sure nothing has shifted is a good idea.

4 – For a little extra support, a piece of .005 sheet styrene was added to the inside of each side. Using anything thicker will interfere with mounting the shell on the chassis.

If you started this process in the evening, it is probably now 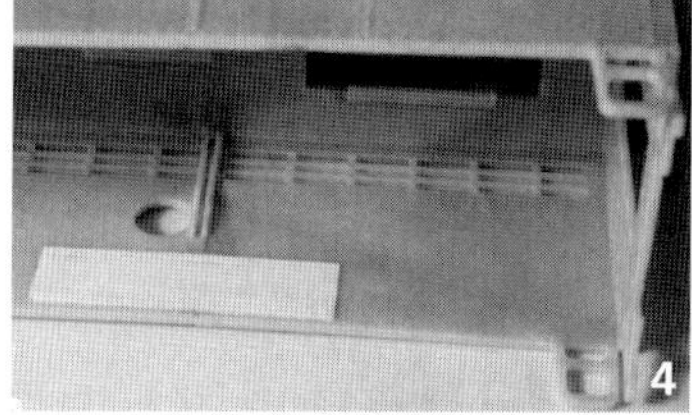 the wee hours of the morning, so set it aside and go to bed. The rest can wait.

Finishing Adjustments

In theory, if everything has been done right up to now the job would be finished except perhaps for some light polishing on the curved portion where the walls join the roof. So much for theory. Careful examination with my Optivisor revealed areas that needed some attention — heights slightly off, gaps in some of the thin raised areas around the grille housing and bottom rivet strip, etc. Correcting these imperfections was done using a combination of the tools and supplies listed above. Putty was added where necessary; a toothpick was used to smooth seam lines adjacent to the rivet panels; the seam scraper was used to remove larger misalignments and the sanding sticks were used to smooth that curved portion above the walls.

There is a raised vertical lip at the former front end of the grille housing by the joint that must be filed down so the longer grilles necessary for

Table 2 — Build Dates of UP E8 and E9 Units

(Table compiled from E8/E9 roster data presented by Gary Binder in his article "Union Pacific Racehorses — E-8 and E-9 Diesels" in *The Streamliner*, Vol. 2, No. 2, April 1986.)

Model	A Unit Nos.	B Unit Nos.	Build Date	Notes
E8	926	926B	5/50	1, 2
	927	927B	6/50	1, 2
	928	928B	7/50	1, 2
	929, 930	929B, 930B	8/50	1, 2
	925		1/52	2
		922B, 931B-937B	2/53	
	931-933	923B, 924B, 938B-944B	3/53	2
	934-938	925B, 945B-949B	4/53	2
	939-942		5/53	2
E9	943-945	950B-955B	5/54	
	946, 947	956B-959B	6/54	
	948-950	960B-962B	5/55	
	951-953	963B-964B	6/55	
	954, 955	965B, 966B	7/55	
	957		9/55	
	956, 958-961	967B-974B	10/55	
	962		11/55	
	904-906	900B, 901B, 903B	1/56	3
	903	902B, 904B	2/56	3
	900-902		5/56	3
	907		6/56	3
	908, 909		9/61	3
	910, 911	910B, 911B	12/62	
	912	912B, 913B	12/63	
	913, 914		1/64	

NOTES

1) E8A 926-930 and E8B 926B-930B were the only UP units equipped with 36″ dynamic-brake fans and horizontal grilles. All other E8s and E9s had 48″ dynamic-brake fans and Farr vertical grilles.

2) E8As were originally equipped with two 2,500-lbs./hr. steam generators. Most were replaced over the years with a single 4,000-lbs./hr. steam generator (according to Binder 931, 940 and 942 apparently ended up with just one 2,500 lbs./hr. steam generator). All E8B units and all E9s came factory-equipped with a single 4,000-lbs./hr. steam generator.

3) UP E9As 900-909 had a second headlight opening in the front door. All other E9As had a single headlight.

the B unit can lie flat. Now is the time to file it down and make sure the grille lies flat over this area.

Dynamic Brakes

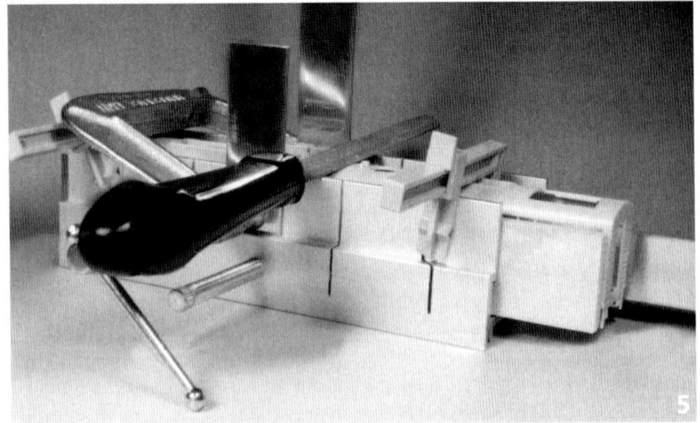

5 — If you are modeling a Union Pacific B unit with dynamic brakes (or unit from any other road that used dynamic brakes) now is the time to add this feature. This was also a rather scary proposition for me since it requires flattening a portion of the roof ⅝″ square for a 48″ dynamic-brake fan (or ½″ for a 36″ fan). I could easily imagine butchering the roof and ruining the project.

This is the jig arrangement I used for flattening a ⅝″ square area in the center roof panel for mounting the 48″ dynamic-brake fan. X-Acto's large mitre box was the perfect height to ensure that the file cut was kept level and didn't go too deep. The Disston file used just happened to be the perfect width. If a narrower file is used, an additional set of vertical guides will be necessary.

6 – After the basic file cut had been made, final sanding was done with Squadron filing sticks (fine and extra-fine). A hole is drilled in the center for the mounting pin of the dynamic-brake fan.

7 – The B unit starts to take form with the addition of some of Life-Like's detail parts and the Details West dynamic-brake fan. The forward roof-panel insert has had its steam-generator details carved off and sanded down. Only the right forward and left rear lift rings are used on this blank panel. To fill the other pre-drilled holes, either glue in Life-Like's lift rings or .020 styrene rod and trim.

8 – The boiler-water fills on B units are located just forward of the second rivet strip on both sides. They were made by filing a taper on DA

1902 air vents. DA 3003 sand-fill hatches have been centered between the second and third rivet strips on a centerline with the portholes. They have also been used to replace the molded-on, late-type sand-fill hatches at the rear (not visible here); this means this model is an E8B. The backup light is a DW 162, and the conduit was formed from .015 phosphor bronze wire.

To more accurately represent the area behind the Farr grilles, .010 x .060 styrene strips were fit between the horizontal grille supports. A NorthWest Short Line chopper makes this job much easier. Refer to the Figure for dimensions of strips and open areas. I chose to remove the supports from the open areas but they could be left in place and painted flat black. You don't have to be too concerned about how level these strips are; the grilles hide these irregularities and only allow the color to show through.

9 – This E9B was detailed just like the E8B except that the late-style DA 3004 sand-fill hatches were used. The pre-drilled holes in the ends for the ladder-type grabs need to be filled with .020 styrene rod. Union Pacific used ladder-support grabs on the roof instead.

On B units, the boiler-water fill on the carbody replaces the forward filler used on the A units. Although this detail should be removed and filled in on a B unit, I chose not to remove it since Life-Like uses these fillers for securing the shell to the chassis.

Paint and Decals

10 — The model is now essentially complete except for the addition of the Farr air grilles. AccuFlex paint and Microscale decals were used on these models. I used Harbor Mist Gray (16-25) as a primer, but I would recommend using a light gray (like SP Letter Gray [16-39]) or even Reefer White (16-02) because of the translucent characteristics of AccuFlex's yellows…the underlying color will make a difference. Because of this, and using my UP color-control cards as a guide, I mixed my own Armour Yellow by mixing equal parts of Armour Yellow (16-24) and Erie Lackawanna Yellow (16-52). The choice on whether to mix colors to match your existing equipment or to use their colors is up to you, but I would strongly recommend using either a white or light-gray primer coat under their Armour Yellow.

After adding the red stripes to one side with Microscale's UP decal stripes (87-110-5) I decided it would be easier to paint the red stripe over the lower rivet strip and just use the decal stripes for the top separator stripe (which is on the smooth surface just above the rivet strip). Signal Red (16-07) is a perfect match.

Road numbers are on the front sides of the units only. Refer to specific prototype photos for correct placement of lettering — UP didn't always follow their painting diagrams. Based on the photos I've seen, the spacing on the Union Pacific lettering for the FM units on the 87-109 decal sheet is closer to what it should be for the E8/9s than the ones Microscale says are for the E8/9s. The builder's plates are located on the

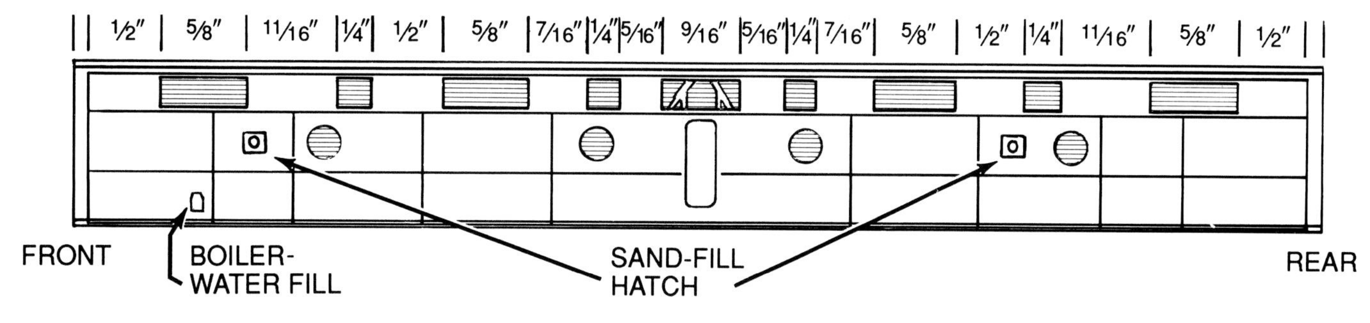

fuel skirting just forward of the center ladder. Refer to photos for the position (or presence) of Lessor plates.

The trucks were painted Santa Fe Silver (16-32) after a primer coat of Harbor Mist Gray. I airbrushed the trucks in place after "masking" the frame with a piece of paper. Any overspray that gets on the wheels can be removed with Kadee's® loco driver cleaner. A comment about the trucks is in order here. Life-Like has designed these trucks so that the journals actually move up and down with the axles. The brake shoes are cast onto a separate "jointed" black piece that fits behind the sideframes and also allows them to move up and down with the wheels. Since both the sideframes and brake-shoe assemblies need to be painted silver, it is easiest to spray it all and then use flat black to paint the flat areas of the brake-shoe assemblies.

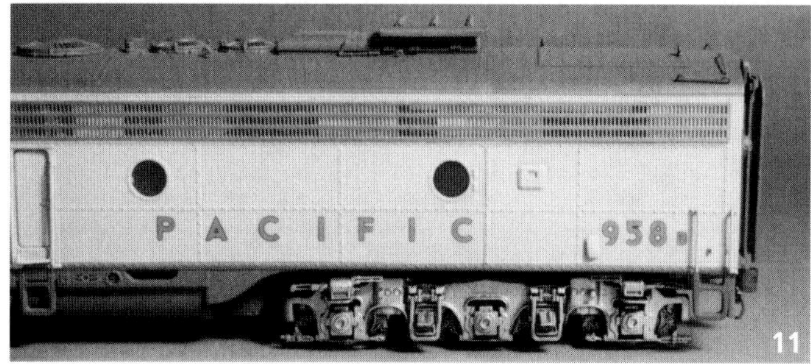

11 – UP E9B 958B has the snow shields (Utah Pacific 83) which started appearing in 1956. This close-up view shows the added Farr grille and where the joint was made between the two shells.

To make the extra-length grille required for a B unit, a third piece of grille must be used. Although Life-Like's grille isn't as fine as those by Detail Associates, the DA grilles are too wide for use here. To get as near perfect a match as possible, I laid one grille on top of the other and slid one until I had the correct grille length. By holding the grilles up to the light, a perfect alignment of the grooves can be made; note that there is definitely a front and back side to these grilles. The two grilles were then taped together to ensure alignment and a heavy pair of scissors was used to cut through both grilles near the end of one. On a Farr grille, make the cut between a pair of vertical bars. On a horizontal grille, make the cut between the double vertical bars.

I used a light spray of 3M's Super 77 spray adhesive on the backs of the grilles to provide a tacky surface for accurate positioning of the grilles. I then peeled up one end and applied a slow-setting CA for a permanent bond. After that end had dried in place, I repeated the process on the other end. I chose to splice the pieces together at the rear of the unit. Remember that these grilles are not a single piece on the prototype; each is made up of six sections (five on an A unit), so having a seam showing is acceptable…in fact, you might want to add some more.

The only extra details added to the ends were the backup lights (both ends). Since these are operating models that will remain coupled together most of the time, I chose not to add MU hoses.

12 – Here an unmodified pre-production UP E8A 928 is seen with my kitbashed E9B 958B. Note the more prototypical appearance behind the grille area on the B unit. Note also how the black brake shoes get lost on the A unit.

E8 939B is a circa-1956 unit ready for service.

E9 958B, also a circa-1956 unit, has already had its snow shields added by the boys in the shop.

Chassis Modifications

The only modifications required on the chassis are the removal of the cab interior and the constant directional lighting (or constant directional/Mars light) circuitry. Removal of the entire cab interior is accomplished by unscrewing the two screws that attach the entire assembly to the chassis. They are located just behind the cab's back wall. The front portion of the cab interior is spot-glued to the vertical post just forward of the crewmen. A slight twist will loosen for removal. Do not detach the wiring yet.

Two screws hold both types of circuit boards. By removing the circuit board and leaving it connected to the bulb(s) in the cab, you can easily reinstall this unit in another engine at some later time. Detaching the power leads is slightly different depending on which module your engine is equipped with.

▼ Mars light/constant lighting unit — If you have the module with the Mars light, cut the two red and two blue power leads coming from the trucks about ¾″ from the circuit board. DO NOT CUT THE RED LEAD GOING TO THE HEADLIGHT! Cut the black lead that connects the circuit board to the motor about ¾″ from the circuit board. The entire lighting circuit can now be removed. Strip the ends of the two blue leads and the black lead and solder together and insulate with tape. Now strip, solder and insulate the ends of the two red leads.

▼ Constant lighting unit — If your chassis has only the constant lighting circuit, cut the two red leads coming from the trucks and the yellow lead going to the motor about ¾″ from the circuit board. Strip, solder all three ends together and insulate.

Test run your chassis to make sure your connections are made properly.

I recommend using Life-Like's dummy knuckle couplers between units to keep the proper spacing between units and the diaphragms snug. Even Kadee's shortest-shanked couplers are too long.

Conclusion/Addendum

As I mentioned earlier, this was my first attempt at cutting and splicing shells. It only requires average skills, but having the right tools and patience are mandatory. Since these two were done, I have done five more in live-demonstration clinics. If I can do it under these circumstances, you most certainly can too.

In doing the additional units I have also found better methods for installing the dynamic-brake fans and doing the solid panels behind the air-intake grilles.

For 36″ dynamics, I remove a square panel and fan from a cannibalized shell, first rough cutting it out, then carefully sanding it down to the panel edges. After masking off where the panel should go with masking tape and scoring its outline, I use a Dremel and a ⅛″ drill bit to roughly rout out the hole. The hole is trued using sanding sticks and a file, checking regularly to ensure a perfect fit. By modifying this technique and using some sheet styrene and the see-through PS 3993 fan you can do the same for the 48″ fan.

A better way to do the solid panels behind the grilles is to remove the grille supports and then cement in panels where indicated in the Figure; don't remove the angled or straight center supports above the doors. To make the panels, increase the width of a strip of Evergreen ³/₁₆″ channel (#266) by .025; do this by cementing a strip of .010 x .060 (#103) to one edge and a strip of .015 x .060 (#113) to the other edge. Use a NWSL Chopper to cut each panel to length (make as many of

each length needed before changing setting). Don't remove more than about 3″ of the grille support at a time or the sidewalls will become quite flimsy. I've also switched over to using Heun's Moveable Model Glue for attaching the grilles.

Acknowledgements

I wish to thank Terry Metcalfe, Gary Binder, Bill Metzger and A. J. Wolff for their assistance. ▮

Bill of Materials

Manufacturer	Part No.	Description
Life-Like	8129	Undecorated powered E8 (comes with both types of grilles, pilots and steam-generator panels)
Creative Model Associates	1102	.015 phosphor bronze wire (roof grabs and backup light conduit)
Detail Associates	1902	Flat air vents (taper to represent boiler water fill)
	2206	Eyebolts, formed wire
	2215	Grabiron, cab ladder
	3003	EMD early cab unit sand hatch (for E8)
	3004	EMD late cab unit sand hatch (for E9)
Details West	162	Pyle-type backup light
	143	48″ cab-top dynamic-brake fan* or
Precision Scale	3993	48″ cab-top dynamic-brake fan (see-through)
Microscale	87-48	Diesel loco data
	87-109	UP passenger cabs
	87-110-5	UP stripes
	MC-4056	EMD and GE loco builder's plates
MV Products	25	Lenses (backup lights)
Utah Pacific	83	UP snow shields

If your local dealer isn't willing to order the following necessary parts, you can order them by sending a check or money order to: Life-Like, Products, Inc., ATTN: Dock 2, 1600 Union Ave., Baltimore, MD 21211. Add 10% for postage and handling. MD residents add 5% sales tax.

Qty.	Part No.	Description	Price
1	584700	E8 body shell	15.00
1	584712	Farr vertical and standard horizontal grilles (2 ea.)	5.00
1	584714	Body detail parts Package 2	15.00

*E8As 926-930 and E8Bs 926B-930B had 36″ dynamic-brake fans — use one of the Life-Like's fans hidden under the winterization hatch.